Made in USA

Creator, Creative Director, Writer- Wesley Smoot

Photography by Adrian Lopez

Recipes by Jehn Ngo

Art Direction by Nathan Rhys Córdoba

Title Design by Christoph Michaud

Copy Editing by Troy Stacha

Distribution by Seattle Book Company

WESLO PUBLISHING

We could all use an extra hand. In the kitchen, that is. So when it comes to reaching out (or around) for that help, I encourage you to pick up your copy of WESLO's HOME-O-EROTIC COOKBOOK.

Delicious Men. Delicious Recipes. A motto we live by. And while we don't encourage you personally to cook naked, we do want you to experiment. So keep an open mind. I heard you already do. We all heard.

We're certain you'll appreciate the variety of scrumptious dishes we have awaiting you. Whether it's a ginger bear making ginger bears, daddies tossing salad, or beefcakes grilling steak, there's something for everyone's unique taste in WESLO's HOME-O-EROTIC COOKBOOK.
And if you're easily offended by swear words, language of a sexual nature, homosexuals, humor, or the human body, we look forward to your feedback.

Please send all thoughts, concerns, and hate-mail to:
bye-felicia@home-o-erotic.com

WESLO'S
Home Erotic
COOKBOOK

"My weaknesses have always been food and men. In that order."

— Dolly Parton

Good morning, bitches! Is there anything better than waking up to a delicious, homemade breakfast? I can think of a few things.

But in case you're not fortunate enough to have breakfast awaiting your welcome to the world, here's a few recipes that are sure to get you going.

After all, breakfast is the most important meal of the day, and the truth is, all men awake with an appetite for something. Don't believe me? Just look under the covers next time you rise. It's hard not to notice. It's right in front of you. Your stomach, give it what it's craving.

Rise and Shine

BLUEBERRY MUFFINS

Serving Size: 12

What's sweet and tart? Not your favorite cocktail, hooker. By the way it's a bit early for that. These muffins are one of our favorite recipes. Perfect for when you're on the go, and great to share with friends. And while it may be too early for a cocktail, perhaps a mimosa in the meantime?

1	stick unsalted, sweet cream butter
2 1/2	c AP flour
2	tsp baking powder
1	tsp baking soda
1/2	tsp salt
1	tsp ground cinnamon
	pinch of nutmeg
1/2	c buttermilk
1	c sour cream
2	ea eggs
1	ea vanilla bean, scraped
1	lemon, zested on microplane
2	c blueberries (fresh or frozen)

TOPPING

3	tbsp unsalted, sweet cream butter, chilled and cubed
1/2	c AP flour
4	tbsp brown sugar

1. Preheat oven to 350°F.

2. In a stainless steel sauce pan, melt 1 stick of butter on low heat. Cook until milk solids separated and start to brown in the bottom of the pan. Butter will take on a nutty note. Set aside to cool slightly.

3. While butter cools, sift all dry ingredients into a large mixing bowl.

4. Combine all wet ingredients in a separate bowl, including the vanilla and lemon zest.

5. Pour wet mix into dry mix and stir until batter starts to come together but still streaky. Stir in browned butter, and gently fold in blueberries

FOR THE TOPPING

1. In a bowl, whisk brown sugar into flour. Use a pastry blender or fork to cut the cold butter into the flour until a crumbly mixture comes together.

2. Fill a greased muffin tin with batter. Top with streusel topping, and bake for 15 to 18 minutes or until tops are browned and toothpick inserted into center comes out clean.

BUTTERMILK PANCAKES

Serving Size: 6 - 8

Delicious, built for your mouth, and paired with nuts. You guessed it, banana walnut pancakes. These little cakes are packed with flavor and crunch. Best drizzled with something sweet.

1 3/4	c AP flour
2 1/2	tsp baking powder
1/2	tsp baking soda
1/4	c sugar
1/2	tsp salt
2	c buttermilk
2	ea eggs
1	ea vanilla bean, scraped
1	ea lemon, juiced
1/4	c melted butter
1	c clarified butter for griddle
	maple syrup

1. In a bowl, sift dry ingredients.

2. In a separate bowl, whisk together buttermilk, eggs, vanilla, and lemon juice.

3. Make a well in dry ingredients and pour wet mix in until batter almost comes together. Add melted butter and whisk.

4. Heat griddle or large sauté pan on med heat. Add a tbsp of clarified butter and swirl around.

5. Ladle on batter and cook until bubbles rise to top. Flip when bottom of pancake is golden brown.

6. Serve with warm maple syrup.

   Clarified butter will produce a pancake with a nice crust on the outside while giving it a buttery taste. Top with sliced bananas and walnuts.

CREAM CHEESE STUFFED FRENCH TOAST

Serving Size: 4

Stuffed first thing in the morning? You read my mind.

- **4** ea slices of Pullman-style bread, sliced 1" thick
- **4** oz cream cheese, softened
- **2** tbsp caramel sauce or fruit jam
- **6** ea large eggs, beaten
- **1** c milk
- **1** ea vanilla bean, scraped
- **3** tbsp sugar
- **1** tbsp cinnamon, ground
- **1 1/2** c cornflakes
- powdered sugar for dusting
- pinch of nutmeg

1. In a food processor, pulse cornflakes and set aside.

2. Cut each slice of bread in half on the diagonal. Use a small knife to create a pocket for the filling.

3. Preheat oven to 375°F.

4. With a hand mixer, beat cream cheese until fluffy. Fold in caramel or jam.

5. Transfer to a piping bag, fill pockets and refrigerate for 15 minutes.

6. In a large shallow baking dish, combine eggs, milk, vanilla, sugar, cinnamon, and nutmeg.

7. Dip stuffed bread into egg mixture for 10 seconds. Flip and let soak for another 10 seconds.

8. Press into cornflakes and sear on a buttered griddle to brown each side.

9. Transfer to a baking sheet. Repeat with remaining slices.

10. Bake for 4 to 6 minutes. Dust with powdered sugar.

11. Serve with warm maple syrup and nuts if desired.

CINNAMON ROLL FRENCH TOAST

Serving Size: 8

The mixed ones are always the hottest. Can you say, "best of both worlds?"

---

8 stale, day old giant cinnamon rolls (fresh or store bought), halved lengthwise
5 ea eggs
1 c milk
1/4 c granulated sugar
1 vanilla bean, scraped
1 tsp ground cinnamon
maple syrup
toasted pecans *(optional)*

1. In a bowl, whisk eggs, milk, sugar, vanilla and cinnamon. Pour into a shallow baking dish.

2. Dip cinnamon rolls into mix and soak each side for 30 seconds.

3. Heat griddle or large sauté pan on medium heat. Cook in two batches until each side is golden brown.

4. Drizzle warm maple syrup over and top with pecans.

ALL IN BANANA NUT MINI MUFFINS

Serving Size: 24 mini muffins

1/2 c instant oats, ground in a blender
1 1/2 c AP flour
1 1/2 tsp baking powder
1/2 tsp baking soda
1/4 tsp salt
1/4 tsp cinnamon
pinch of nutmeg
1 c overripe bananas
1/3 c applesauce
1/2 c light brown sugar, packed
1 ea large egg
1 tsp vanilla extract
3 tbsp oil
1/4 c blueberries (fresh, frozen, or dried)
1/4 c chopped walnuts
1/4 c mini chocolate chips

1. Preheat oven to 350°F.

2. Lightly grease mini muffin pan.

3. Sift together dry ingredients.

4. Blend together bananas, applesauce, brown sugar, egg, vanilla, and oil.

5. Add wet into dry ingredients in batches.

6. Fold in blueberries, nuts, and chocolate.

7. Bake for 10 to 12 minutes or until toothpick inserted comes out clean.

EGGS BENEDICT

Serving Size: 5

Eggs and ham for your protein. English muffins for your carbs, but I would suggest a side of fruit for some antioxidants. Also because you're a big fruit... love you!

---

4 qts water
1/4 c distilled white vinegar
1 tsp salt
10 ea eggs

HOLLANDAISE SAUCE

3 ea egg yolks
1 ea lemon, juiced
1/4 c hot water, with 1 tbsp kosher salt dissolved
1/4 tsp cayenne pepper
1 lb unsalted, sweet cream butter to yield 2
2 clarified butter
5 ea English muffins, toasted
10 slices of Canadian bacon

1. Melt 1 lb of butter in a small saucepan on low. Cook until milk solids separate and butter oil is clarified. Reserve 2 c of clarified butter. Set aside and keep warm.

2. In a blender, add yolks and lemon juice. Blend on medium until pale in color and doubled in size.

3. Slowly drizzle in 1/2 c of warm clarified butter. Add 1 tbsp of water solution.

4. On high speed, drizzle another 1/2 c butter and then 2 more tbsp of water solution.

5. Add cayenne. Drizzle in last cup of butter, and end with last tbsp of water solution.

6. Sauce should be light and fluffy. Transfer to a thermos to keep warm and prevent from breaking. (The oil separates and sauce becomes flat and watery)

7. In a large sauce pan, bring 4 qts of water to a boil. Add vinegar and drop to a simmer.

8. Swirl the water with a spoon to create a vortex. Crack an egg in one at a time. The vortex should force the egg to form into a round shape. Cook for 4 to 5 minutes and remove with a slotted spoon.

9. To build your eggs benedict, start with a toasted E nglish muffin. Top with one slice of Canadian bacon, poached egg and finish with hollandaise.

OMELETTE

Serving Size: 4

Who came first? Unless you're straight, who cares? You're gonna get yours. And that means cracking a few eggs if you have to. Wait, what are we even talking about anymore? Oh yeah, eggs, and The Southern Belle Omelette. This yummy protein packed omelette mixed with veggies has everything you need to start your day off right, ensuring that you and your health comes first.

---

12 ea eggs
4 tbsp milk
4 tbsp butter
TT kosher salt & black pepper
1 ea red onion, diced
1 ea red bell pepper, diced
2 c mushrooms, sliced
1 c green onion, sliced
1 c cooked breakfast sausage

1. In a small bowl, whisk together 3 eggs, 1 tbsp of milk and a pinch of salt and pepper.

2. Using a small, nonstick sauté pan on medium heat, toss in 1 tbsp of butter and sauté 4 tbsp of mushrooms, and a tbsp each of onion and red bell pepper. Add a pinch of salt and pepper.

3. Sauté for 30 seconds. Add sausage and green onion, and sauté for another 15 seconds.

4. Pour eggs in and swirl pan to distribute evenly. Cook until outer edge is set. Using a rubber spatula, run under the edge of egg, lifting half of the omelette up while tilting the pan to allow uncooked egg to run under omelette. Repeat on other side. Keep doing this until no more uncooked egg run freely in the pan.

5. Flip omelette over to cook the top side for 5 seconds. Flip back over and add cheese if desired.

6. Remove from heat and slide half of omelette onto plate, folding the other half on top.

7. Repeat for next three omelettes.

CRÊPES

Serving Size: 4

Oh you fancy, huh? We are too. But these lovely dishes require no more effort than your average pancake. Although everyone will be way more impressed than they should be. Kinda like those knock off jeans, huh? Werk it!

---

2 eggs
1/2 c water
1/2 c milk
1/4 tsp salt
2 tbsp melted butter
1 c AP flour

1. Use a large mixing bowl and whisk eggs with milk, water, and melted butter.

2. Add dry ingredients, salt and flour. Continue mixing until smooth.

3. Grease griddle and heat to medium high.

4. Pour one fourth across griddle spreading the batter evenly.

5. Cook each side for up to 2 minutes until golden brown.

6. Top with your favorite fruit purée and whipped cream.

BREAKFAST FUNNEL CAKES

Serving Size: 2 - 4

If you didn't feel like enough of a freak show from last night, we're gonna suggest you start your day with a festive funnel cake. Of course it's not the healthiest way to start your day, but neither was that walk of shame. Just don't do it everyday and you'll be fine. The neighbors are starting to talk.

---

4 c AP flour
1/4 tsp cinnamon, ground
1 tbsp baking powder
1/2 tsp salt
1 c light brown sugar, packed
3 eggs
3 c milk
1 vanilla bean, scraped
oil for frying
powdered sugar for dusting

1. Heat oil to 375°F.

2. In a blender, combine flour, cinnamon, baking powder, salt and sugar. Pulse.

3. Add eggs, milk, and vanilla. Blend on medium speed until combined.

4. When oil is ready, pour 1/2 cup of batter into a funnel over the oil in a circular motion.

5. Fry 2 minutes per side or until golden and crispy. Remove and let absorb on plate topped with paper towel.

6. Dust with powdered sugar and serve with fruit topping if desired.

Lunch, like a quickie, is often a rushed experience that can go unappreciated. And like a quickie you may not be able to savor all the moments involved. Whether it's preparing or consuming. Let's change that.

If you can take the few extra minutes out of your day to make a more memorable experience, I highly recommend the Croque Monsieur. That's a popular sandwich in France, not a sex position. Although, don't quote me, it may very well be both. But, perhaps a quickie is just your style. If that's the case we'll have you covered with a number of mid-day pleasures to grant you immediate satisfaction.

Afternoon Delight

BEEFY CHILI

Serving Size: 6

There's the Beef! And the pork! Red onions, spices, shredded cheddar, and everything else needed to prepare and fill your belly with a hearty home cooked bowl of beefy pleasure.

---

1 lb ground chuck, lean
1 lb chorizo
2 lbs pork shoulder, diced into 1/2" cubes
4 tbsp chili powder
2 tbsp cumin
4 ea garlic cloves, minced
1 ea onion, small dice
1 ea red bell pepper, small dice
1 ea yellow bell pepper, small dice
2 ea jalapeno, seeded and ribs removed, small dice
1 12 oz bottle of stout beer
3 15 oz cans crushed tomatoes
4 c beef stock
TT kosher salt
TT black pepper

1. In a large stock pot on high heat, brown ground beef and pork. Add chili powder and cumin along with a few pinches of salt and pepper.

2. Cook until beef has just a little pink left. Add chorizo and cook for another 3 minutes.

3. Mix in onion, bell peppers, jalapeno, and garlic. Add another pinch of salt and pepper. Cook until veggies are soft, about 10 minutes.

4. Pour in beer and scrape up any brown bits that are stuck at the bottom of the pot.

5. Add tomatoes and beef stock. Turn heat down to medium-low heat and simmer for 3 hours. Stir occasionally. Taste and adjust for seasonings.

6. Top chili with your favorite toppings such as cheddar cheese, onions, sour cream, and green onions.

For added heat, do not remove seeds and ribs from jalapeños before cooking.

HAWAIIAN BURGERS

Serving Size: 8

Aloha bitches! Let's add some sass to your burger with something a little unexpected. Juicy pineapples make this recipe worth dancing and singing over, like watching South Pacific for the 50th time. A little less sad but you get what I'm saying. (For all you nubile twinks who don't follow classic cinema, South Pacific is a musical starring Mitzi Gaynor set in Hawaii)

---

1 lb ground beef
1 lb ground pork
1 tsp ground ginger
1 tsp onion powder
2 tsp garlic powder
8 ea slices of Canadian bacon
8 ea slices of pineapple, fresh or canned
8 ea hamburger buns
  TT kosher salt and black pepper

1. Preheat grill to medium high heat.

2. Combine beef, pork, ginger, onion and garlic powder. Form into 8 patties.

3. Salt and pepper both sides of patties before grilling to desired doneness.

4. Grill pineapple and Canadian bacon just to show grill marks. Top burgers.

5. Add cheese, lettuce, tomatoes, onions, and pickles, if desired.

PATTY MELT

Serving Size: 6

Crispy grilled rye, Swiss cheese, yellow onions, and re-runs of The Golden Girls. Maybe I don't need a boyfriend after all!

---

8 oz ground chuck
1 lb ground pork shoulder
2 cloves garlic, minced
1 ea small shallot, minced
1 japanese panko breadcrumbs
2 ea eggs, beaten
1 tbsp Worcestershire
1 tbsp fresh thyme, chopped
TT kosher salt
TT black pepper
3 tbsp canola oil
1 ea large yellow onion, julienned
1 8 oz pkg baby portabella mushrooms, sliced 1/8" thick
12 ea slices of rye bread
12 ea slices of gruyere cheese
butter for toasting bread

1. In a mixing bowl, combine ground chuck, pork, garlic, shallot, panko, eggs, Worcestershire, and thyme. Mix until combined.

2. Form thin, oval patties the size of the rye bread, and place on a sheet tray. Repeat for remaining mixture. Chill in refrigerator for 15 minutes.

3. As the patties are chilling, heat a medium sized sauté pan on medium high heat. Add canola oil, and tilt pan to coat the surface of the pan evenly. Sauté mushrooms and onions until onions are cooked through and soft. Set pan aside and keep on low.

4. Toast slices of rye in a large sauté pan with butter over medium-high heat until golden. Set aside.

5. Take out patties from fridge and sprinkle both sides with salt and pepper.

6. In the same sauté pan on high heat, sear patties in batches of four. Flip patties over. On two patties, top with onion and mushroom mixture. Then top all four with cheese. Cook until cheese is melted. Layer mushroom and onion patty on top of the other patty that only has cheese. Sandwich between two pieces of toasted rye bread.

7. Repeat for all 6 sandwiches.

MEATY TACOS

Serving Size: 8

I could live off these. Diced steak, white onion, and corn tortillas topped with your favorite cheese. I suggest Monterey Jack. I would also suggest this model make them for me in my kitchen, but one out of two ain't bad.

- **4** ea ribeye steaks
- **1/4** c red wine vinegar
- **1/4** c olive oil
- **1/3** c soy sauce
- **1/4** c Worcestershire sauce
- **2** tbsp lemon juice
- **1/4** tsp hot sauce
- **5** ea garlic cloves, smashed
- **1** ea small shallot, rough chopped
- **2** tbsp dried basil
- **1** tbsp dried oregano
- **10** sprigs fresh thyme
- **1** tbsp black pepper
- **1** pkg corn or flour tortillas

1. In a large zip plastic bag, combine all ingredients except for the tortillas.

2. Marinate for 4 hours, up to 24 hours.

3. Pour off marinade and let come to room temperature before grilling.

4. Grill to preferred doneness, let cool for 5 minutes before slicing.

5. Build tacos with meat and any other toppings, if desired.

CHICKEN WRAP

Serving Size: 6

Always wrap it up. And if you're in a hurry, it's all the more important. This is a quick lunch fix that satisfies your hunger and keeps your waistline in check. Lean chicken and greens are the theme of this quickie. Safety first, no regrets.

6	whole wheat tortillas or multigrain flatbread wraps
2 1/2	c rotisserie chicken, de-boned and shredded in large pieces
1	(8 to 10 oz) tub prepared hummus
6	c mixed greens
12	slices ripe roma tomatoes
1	ea lemon, juiced to yield 1 1/2 tbsp
4	tbsp extra virgin olive oil
	TT kosher salt and black pepper

1. Heat tortillas or flatbreads on a large sauté pan on medium heat until warmed through and pliable.

2. Smear on a layer of hummus. Add two slices of tomato to each wrap.

3. In a bowl, toss greens with lemon juice, olive oil, salt, and pepper. Distribute among wraps.

4. Top with chicken and roll like a burrito, folding in the ends. Cut in half before serving.

CROQUE MONSIEUR

Serving Size: 4

Bonjour Mes Amis! What's not to love about the French! The sexy language, tight pants, and pheromones past the point of sexy. Here's one more thing to love. The Croque Monsieur. A delectable change to your average ham and cheese. It takes a little more time but like that French guy that has to tell you about all the things wrong with America before you can take him home, it'll be worth the wait.

2 1/2	c milk
3	tbsp unsalted butter
3	tbsp all purpose flour
1/2	ea small yellow onion, small dice
2	sprigs of thyme
1	ea bay leaf
6	ea peppercorn
4	ea parsley, stems only
1/8	tsp cayenne pepper
	scant pinch of nutmeg
1 1/2	c Gruyere, grated
8	ea 1/2" sliced thick country style bread
8	ea slices of quality ham
4	tbsp clarified butter

1. Preheat oven to 350°F.

2. In a small saucepan, heat milk with onion, thyme, bay, peppercorns and parsley stems on medium heat just until it steams. Do not boil. Strain and reserve.

3. In a medium saucepan, melt 3 tablespoons of butter on medium high heat. When butter is melted, add flour and whisk. Cook until raw flour smell subsides and roux takes on nutty note, about 2 minutes. Whisk in milk and cook until sauce thickens and coats the back of a spoon. Season with salt and pepper and cayenne. Remove from heat.

4. While sauce is still hot, sprinkle in 1/2 c of Gruyere in small batches. (Adding cheese in all at once will result in a grainy sauce.)

5. Brush both sides of bread with clarified butter. Place onto a lined baking sheet and bake for 10 minutes. Remove and turn oven up to 425°F.

6. On one slice of bread, ladle on cheese sauce. spread to outer edges of bread. Top with 2 slices of ham, 1/4 c of gruyere, bread and another ladle of cheese sauce.

7. Bake until golden brown and bubbly. Serve hot.

G U M B O

Serving Size: 6 - 8

Yes please.

- **2** lb medium sized shrimp, shell on, head on (for stock)
- **6** tbsp vegetable oil
- **1/2** c AP flour
- **8** oz andouille sausage, 1/2" slices on a bias
- **1** lb jumbo lump crabmeat
- **3** c fresh okra, sliced 1/4" thick
- **2** c yellow onion, small dice, save scraps for stock
- **1** c celery, small dice, save scraps for stock
- **1** c green bell pepper, small dice
- **1** ea small carrot, for stock
- **2** ea garlic cloves, crushed, for stock
- **4** ea cloves of garlic, minced
- **1** tbsp tomato paste
- **1** c dry white wine
- **10** c cold water
- **6** ea parsley, stems only
- **6** ea sprigs of thyme
- **6** ea black peppercorn
- **1** ea bay leaf
- **1** (28 oz) can of petite diced tomatoes
- **1/2** c green onion, thinly sliced
- **1** lemon, juiced
    TT kosher salt and black pepper
- **3** tbsp cold butter, cubed

1. Peel and devein shrimp. Keep heads and shells for stock. Return shrimp to fridge.

2. In a large stock pot on medium high heat, sauté shrimp shells until pink. Add vegetable scraps, carrot, crushed garlic and cook for 2 more minutes.

3. Add tomato paste and stir, making sure to brown the paste without burning. Deglaze with wine, scraping up all brown bits. Add water, parsley stems, thyme, peppercorns and bay leaf. Bring to a boil and drop to a simmer for 20 minutes. Strain stock and reserve.

4. In a dutch oven on medium high heat, add oil. Heat for 45 seconds then whisk in flour all at once. Turn heat down to medium and cook until roux is a peanut butter color. Add onion, bell pepper, celery and okra. Season with salt and pepper. Sauté for 2 minutes then add minced garlic. Pour in stock and tomatoes. Bring to a boil then drop to a simmer.

5. Add shrimp, sausage and crab and cook until shrimp is no longer opaque, about 15 minutes. Turn off heat.

6. Squeeze in lemon juice. Add green onion and chip in cold butter one piece at a time, making sure the last piece is incorporated before adding the next.

7. Serve over steamed rice.

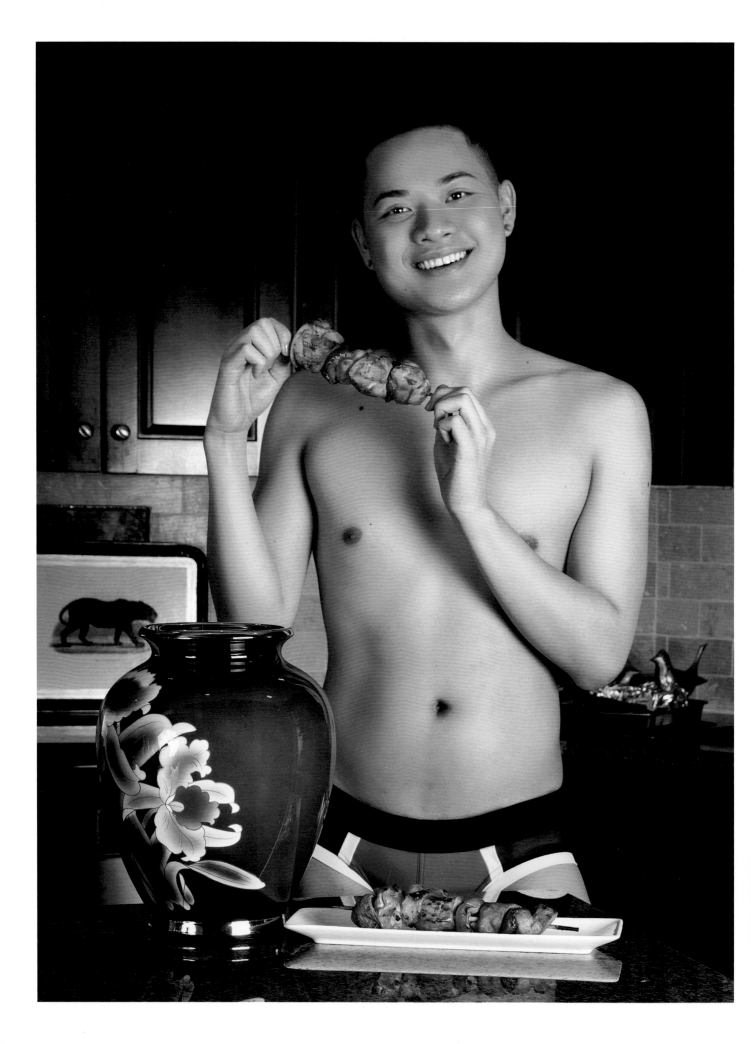

CHICKEN YAKINIKU

Serving Size: 6 - 8

There's lots of ways to prepare Japanese meat. After all, there are few cultures that put so much emphasis on patience. The marinade is the key to unleash the full flavor in this dish, so pretend you have to douche and plan ahead. I prefer this one grilled on a skewer with peppers and onions. And as you can see, young and smooth doesn't hurt either.

8	chicken thighs, skinned and deboned, cut into bite-sized chunks
2	ea red bell pepper, seeds and ribs removed, large dice
2	ea yellow bell pepper, seeds and ribs removed, large dice
2	ea green bell pepper, seeds and ribs removed, large dice
2	ea small red onion, large dice
3/4	c soy sauce
1/2	c sake
1/4	c mirin
1	c granulated sugaar
3	ea cloves of garlic, rough chop
2	oz ginger root, peeled, rough chop
1	tbsp crushed red pepper flakes
1	c green onion, rough chop
1/2	c vegetable oil
1	ea Fuji apple, grated
1	pkg skewers

1. Soak skewers in water. Set aside.

2. In a small saucepan on medium high heat, combine soy, sake, mirin, garlic, ginger, and crushed red pepper. Bring to a boil then drop to a simmer for 2 minutes.

3. Turn off heat, and add green onion. Transfer to a blender on medium speed for 15 seconds. Crank blender to high and slowly drizzle in oil. Pour into a bowl and add apple. Chill.

4. Place chicken chunks in a plastic zip bag. Pour enough marinade to just cover meat. Press out as much air from bag before sealing. Marinate for 2 hours.

5. After the two hours, preheat grill.

6. Remove chicken from marinade and discard marinade. Assemble skewers, alternating chicken with peppers and onion.

7. Grill skewers over medium high heat until chicken is done and juices run clear.

8. Brush on remaining marinade and serve hot.

PORTOBELLO MUSHROOM BURGER

Serving Size: 4

Ain't you a cute little vegetarian? You thought between all these carnivorous meals, we would leave you out. Well we almost did. But we threw in this recipe last minute so now you can totally sit with us! We'll let you annoy waiters on your own time.

MARINADE

1/2	c balsamic vinegar
2	tbsp Worcestershire sauce
2	tbsp garlic, minced
2	tbsp shallots, minced
8	ea fresh thyme sprigs
1	c olive oil
	TT kosher salt and black pepper
4	ea lg portobello caps, stems and gills removed
2	ea red bell peppers, cut into large strips
4	hamburger buns

GARLIC CHIVE AIOLI

2/3	c mayo
1/4	c sour cream
2	tsp garlic, minced
1/2	ea small lemon, juiced
2	tbsp fresh chives, thinly sliced
	TT kosher salt and black pepper

1. In a bowl, combine vinegar, Worcestershire, garlic and shallots. Throw in a pinch of salt and pepper. Slowly whisk in olive oil until emulsified. Add thyme sprigs.

2. Place mushrooms, cap side down in a shallow baking dish, along with bell pepper strips. Pour marinade over and set in refrigerator for 2 hours.

3. Pull mushrooms and peppers from fridge and discard marinade.

4. Preheat grill. Cover a section with foil so the bell peppers do not fall through the grates.

5. For the aioli, mix all ingredients together and set aside.

6. Grill mushrooms over medium heat until tender and slightly charred. Grill peppers on foil side of grill until warmed through.

7. Assemble burgers with garlic chive aioli.

SLOPPY JOES

Serving Size: 8

If you're usually a hot mess when drinking and think you need a change, try our Sloppy Joes. Now you can be a hot mess when you eat. This blend of lean ground beef with brown sugar and spices will make you care less if it gets all over your designer shirt. On second thought, I suggest you take it off.

2	tbsp oil
1	ea green bell pepper, seeded, small dice
1	ea red bell pepper, seeded, small dice
1	large yellow onion, small dice
2	tbsp garlic, minced
1/4	c tomato paste
1 1/2	lb extra lean ground beef
1/2	lb ground pork
1/4	c AP flour
3	tsp chili powder
1/4	tsp cayenne pepper
2	tbsp cider vinegar
2	tbsp Worcestershire sauce
1	tbsp bbq sauce
1/4	c packed brown sugar
2	(15oz) cans tomato sauce
	TT kosher salt and black pepper
8	hamburger buns

1. In a dutch oven on medium heat, sauté peppers and onions until soft. Add garlic and sauté until fragrant. Stir in tomato paste and brown, but do not burn. Turn heat up to medium high and cook ground beef and pork until no longer pink. Season with salt and pepper, chili powder, and cayenne. Sprinkle flour over and stir, cooking for another 3 minutes.

2. Combine vinegar, Worcestershire, BBQ sauce, and brown sugar. Add to the meat mixture, along with the two cans of tomato sauce. Bring to a boil then drop to a simmer for 35 to 40 minutes, stirring occasionally. Taste and adjust seasonings.

3. Sloppy joes are ready to assemble, though the flavor is much better if you wait a day to eat it. The flavors will meld together overnight in the fridge. Freeze any leftovers for up to 6 months.

SOUP & SAMMIE

Serving Size: 4 - 6

Maybe I do need a partner! You two are just the cutest pair I've ever seen. You have been together forever and complement each other so well. I could just eat you both up. And I think I will! Put aside the processed cheese and canned soup. Like any relationship, or recipe worth the damn, it takes time and work. But in the end, it's always worth it.

ROASTED YELLOW TOMATO SOUP

- **8** ea large yellow tomatoes, quartered
- **4** ea cloves of garlic, smashed
- **1** bunch of fresh thyme sprigs
- **1/4** c olive oil
- **2** ea yellow bell peppers
- **1** ea small carrot, small dice
- **2** ea celery, small dice
- **1** ea large yellow onion, small dice
- **2** c chicken stock
- **1** ea bay leaf
- **1/4** c heavy cream
  cherry tomatoes, quartered, for garnish
  TT kosher salt and black pepper

BOURSIN GRILLED CHEESE

- **8** ea thick slices of sour dough bread
- **8** tbsp unsalted butter
- **8** ea slices of white cheddar
- **1** ea block of Boursin cheese, any flavor

1. Preheat oven to 425°F.

2. For the tomato soup, line a sheet tray with parchment paper and lay the quartered tomatoes and crushed garlic on it. Drizzle with olive oil and sprinkle with salt and pepper. Scatter thyme spigs over the tomatoes. Roast for 10 to 15 minutes until tomatoes are soft. Discard thyme sprigs.

3. While the tomatoes roast, lightly coat bell peppers with oil and char over open flame on a gas stove burner, turning to char all sides. Transfer to a zip plastic bag to let steam for easily removing skin. Alternately, if you have an electric stove, this can be done in the same oven for the tomatoes. Roast until the outside is browned and transfer to a zip plastic bag to steam for 5 minutes. Remove charred skin and de-seed. Set aside.

4. In a dutch oven over medium heat, sweat the carrot, celery, and onion until soft. Add roasted tomatoes, garlic, bell peppers, chicken stock, and bay leaf. Bring to a boil and drop to a simmer for 30 mins. Remove bay leaf. Use a blender or immersion stick to puree the soup. Push soup through a fine mesh strainer to remove tomato skins and seeds. Pour into a clean pot and heat with cream. Taste and adjust seasonings. Top with cherry tomatoes.

5. For the grilled cheese, using a griddle on medium heat, melt 4 tbsp of butter. Toast the bread on one side until golden. Flip over and toast the other side with the other 4 tbsp of butter. On four slices of toasted bread, lay two slices of white cheddar. The other four slices with get the Boursin cheese spread. Combine one cheddar side with one Boursin side, cheese side inside. Heat on griddle until cheese is melted and bread is toasted. Cut into triangles and serve with tomato soup.

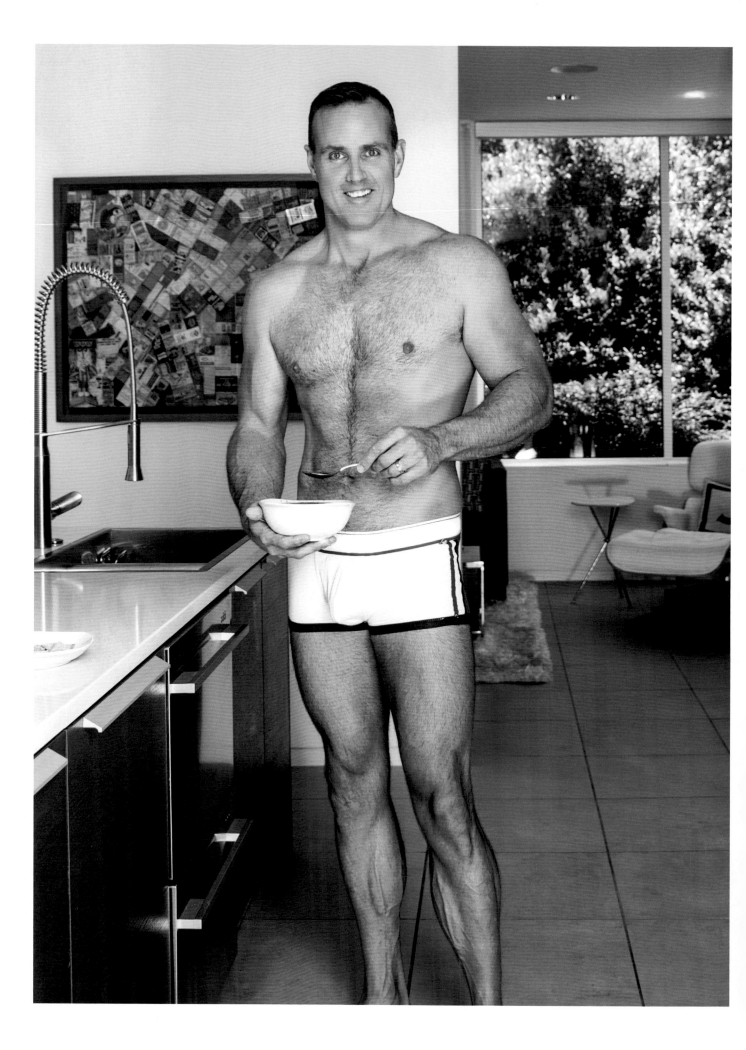

VEGGIE SOUP

Serving Size: 6 - 8

Eat your veggies and you'll grow up big and strong like all of those homoerotic action figures you played with as a kid. Could one aspire for more? "Look mom, all done!"

---

4 tbsp oil
1 yellow onion, small diced
6 ea garlic cloves, minced
1 c dry white wine
2 ea (32oz) container of vegetable stock
2 lbs russet potatoes, scrubbed and sliced into 1/4" rounds, skin on
2 ea (15oz) cans of cannellini beans, drained
1 tsp dried oregano
1 tsp dried basil
1 tbsp fresh rosemary, finely chopped
1 tsp crushed red pepper flakes
8 c kale, zipped, rough chopped
TT kosher salt and black pepper

1. In a dutch oven on medium-high heat, add oil. Swirl to cover surface of pot. Add onions and sweat until soft and translucent.

2. Add garlic and cook until fragrant. De-glaze with white wine. Add stock, beans, potatoes, herbs, and pepper flakes. Sprinkle with salt and pepper.

3. Bring soup to a boil then drop to a simmer. Cover and cook for 10 to 12 minutes or until potatoes are done but not falling apart. Add kale and cook for another 5 minutes.

4. Taste and adjust seasonings.

There are few more pleasing experiences than tossing a fresh salad. Ain't that the truth! Food critic Gael Greene once said, "Great food is like great sex, the more you have, the more you want." So use this chapter to keep your guests wanting more and more. Keep in mind, first impressions are everything. Now wet your lips, teasing is half the fun.

Foreplay

GINGER SPICE SALAD

Serving Size: 6

In this recipe Ginger has a lot of soul. Combined with the robust taste of mango and golden raisins, it will leave you less concerned about if the carpet matches the drapes in this photo, and more concerned with where it all went. By the way, where do gingers go when they die? Love 'em while you can!

DRESSING

1/4	c golden raisins
1	c white wine
3	tbsp wine vinegar
2	tsp honey
1	tsp Dijon mustard
1	tsp ginger root, minced
1	ea small jalapeño, de-seeded and minced
1/4	c olive oil
1	tbs cilantro leaves, rough chopped
	TT kosher salt

SALAD

6	c mixed greens
1	c cilantro leaves, loosely packed
1	ea ripe mango, cut into chunks
1	ea red bell pepper, julienned
	TT kosher salt and black pepper

1. Soak raisins in white wine overnight, drain, and set aside.

2. In a blender purée raisins.

3. Add vinegar, honey, mustard, ginger, jalapeño, and cilantro.

4. Blend well. Season with salt.

5. Slowly drizzle in oil while blender is still running.

6. Taste and adjust with more salt or vinegar if needed.

7. Combine mixed greens and cilantro in large salad bowl.

8. Add bell pepper, mango, a pinch of salt and pepper.

9. Drizzle dressing over salad.

10. Lightly toss to coat salad.

11. Serve immediately.

MAJOR'S TOSSED SALAD

Serving Size: 4

Don't think about the smell. Just go right in!
Because if you think it about it too much, the smell of feta cheese is enough to put anyone off.
Prepared correctly, feta cheese can add the perfect spark to any tossed salad. We also added chopped bacon, diced avocados, onions, and croutons for crunch.
Now pour your favorite vinaigrette and toss, toss, toss!

- **8** c mixed greens
- **5** oz olive oil and balsamic vinaigrette
- **1/3** c feta cheese
- **1/4** c sunflower seeds
- **1** large avocado diced
- **1/2** large white onion diced
- **1/2** c cooked bacon, chopped
  garlic croutons

1. Combine mixed greens, onions, sunflower seeds and avocado in large mixing bowl.

2. Add vinaigrette and toss thoroughly.

3. Add feta cheese and bacon, continue tossing.

4. Top with croutons and serve.

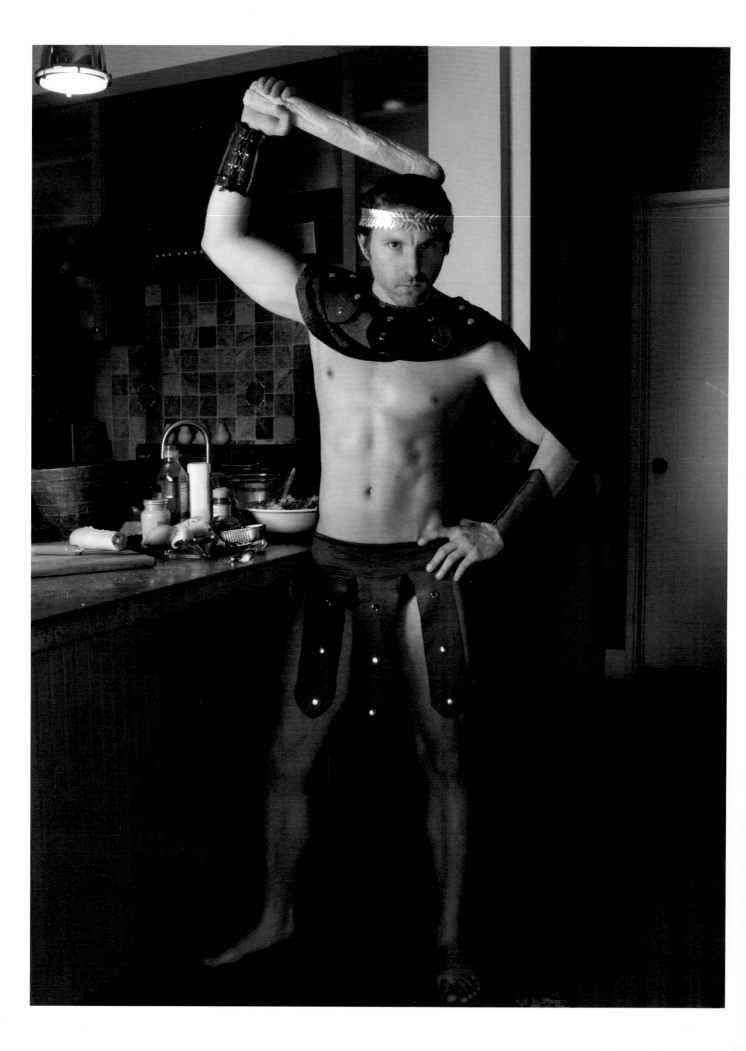

GRILLED CAESAR SALAD

Serving Size: 4

Aww Hell! It's time we All Hail Caesar salad in all its glory. Creamy sauce, rich flavor, and what can't parmesan cheese make better? Did you know traditional caesar salad is topped with diced anchovies? So if the smell of fish doesn't make you too squeamish perhaps you'll want to experiment like you almost did in high school. The smell on your breath will make your dad so proud. Ok, I'll stop.

DRESSING
- **3** ea garlic cloves, peeled and smashed
- **4** ea anchovy fillets, rinsed and patted dry
- **1** ea egg yolk
- **2** tbsp fresh lemon juice
- **1 1/2** tsp Worcestershire
- **1/2** tsp hot sauce, such as Tabasco
- **3** tbsp parmesan cheese, finely grated or microplaned
- **1/4** c olive oil
- TT kosher salt
- TT black pepper

SALAD
- **2** ea romaine hearts, halved, cores intact
- **4** ea parmesan crisps, recipe follows

1. Preheat oven to 350°F. Line a baking sheet with a silicone mat or parchment paper coated with nonstick spray. Divide 2 ounces of grated parmesan into 4 mounds. Lightly pat down with fingers. Bake cheese until melted and lightly golden, about 6 to 8 minutes. Transfer to wire rack. While parmesan is still warm, you can use a cookie cutter round to punch out perfect circles. Alternatively, you can cut crisps into triangles or strips using a bench knife or butter knife. *Do not use a sharp knife to cut on silicone mats. If using a sharp knife, transfer crisps to cutting board before cutting.* Set aside.

2. In a food processor or blender, combine garlic, anchovies, egg yolk, and lemon juice. Pulse until smooth. Add Worcestershire, hot sauce, parmesan, and a pinch of salt and pepper. While food processor or blender is still going, slowly drizzle in olive oil until combined.

3. Heat a lightly oiled grill pan over medium-high heat until hot but not smoking. Grill romaine hearts on grill until lightly charred, about 3 to 5 minutes, Sprinkle with salt and pepper. Transfer to serving dish.

4. Drizzle caesar dressing over romaine hearts. Place crisps around and between romaine hearts.

BACON WRAPPED JALAPEÑOS

Serving Size: 12

Muy calienté! No, what he's holding. That's still not his hand! Well fine, but when you finally decide to look up you'll see halved jalapeños filled with cream cheese, wrapped in bacon, and a hot Mexican hunk in his skivvies eating jalapeños in the Texas sun. Think of something hotter, I bet you can't.

12 halved jalapeño pepper
2 packages cream cheese
24 slices of bacon
24 toothpicks

1. Take halved jalapeños and spoon enough cream cheese to fit each half without overfilling.

2. Wrap each half in a piece of raw bacon and set aside until all 24 are complete.

3. You can choose to grill the jalapeños on foil at low heat for 15 minutes on each side or bake them at 275 degrees for 1 hour or until bacon is fully cooked.

4. Mixing small diced green onion into the cream cheese can add some yummy flavor

CHEESE BOATS

Serving Size: 24

When I first heard this recipe I thought, "Okay white people, you need to stop! You can't just put mayonnaise on everything." Yet I stand corrected. This is a delightful little finger food that will make you agree that if you're persistent enough, you're bound to get it right every once in a while. I'm just kidding white people.

---

3 shredded medium cheddar
6 chopped green onions
1 c mayonnaise
1 c chopped pecans
2 fl oz of jalapeño peach preserves
24 pastry boats

1. Mix all ingredients together in a bowl and refrigerate overnight.

2. Scoop cheese mixture evenly into pastry boats.

3. Serve cold on tray.

4. Use crackers if pastry boats cannot be easily found.

MAMA'S HOT SAUCE

Serving Size: 6

This is my mama's recipe that I absolutely love and absolutely had to feature in our book. She is my world and my light. Sorry the model has a hard on, moms. Love you always!

---

4 fl oz of water
1/2 tbsp sea salt
1 tooth of garlic
4 fire roasted serrano peppers
6 fire roasted roma tomatoes

1. Cut stems end of jalapeños off at about a 1/4"

2. Once cooled peel tomatoes.

3. Combine all ingredients into blender.

4. Blend for 1 minute.

5. Add additional tomatoes if too spicy.

6. Hey, some like it Hot!

GUACAMOLE

Serving Size: 4 - 5

---

5 ea ripe avocados
1 ea small red onion, small dice
2 ea roma tomatoes, seeded and small dice
ea garlic cloves, minced
2 ea jalapeno, seeds and ribs removed,
1 minced
1/4 c chopped cilantro
1 ea lime, juiced
TT kosher salt and black pepper

1. Scoop out flesh from avocados.

2. Add onion, tomatoes, garlic, jalapeno, cilantro, and lime juice.

3. Season with salt and pepper.

4. Enjoy with tortilla chips.

OLIVE, SUN DRIED TOMATOES, & GOAT CHEESE CANAPE

Serving Size: 24pcs

1/2	pkg phyllo (filo) dough sheets, thawed
4	tbsp unsalted, sweet cream butter, melted
1	c kalamata olives, rough chopped
1	c sun dried tomatoes, rough chopped
5	ea garlic cloves, minced
16	oz cream cheese, room temperature
8	oz goat cheese room temperature
1	tbsp fresh oregano, chopped
1	tsp fresh thyme leaves
1	ea lemon, zested
1	tbsp basil chiffonade

1. Preheat oven to 350°F.

2. In a mixer with a paddle attachment, whip cream cheese with goat cheese.

3. Fold herbs and zest into cheese. Transfer to a pastry bag.

4. Brush phyllo sheets with melted butter, and cut into 2 1/2" squares.

5. In a lightly greased mini muffin pan, layer 3 squares of phyllo dough in each well, making sure each layer overlaps the previous at a different angle.

6. Gently press down to create a pastry cup.

7. Bake for 8 to 10 minutes or until dough in flaky and golden. Let cool.

8. In a food processor, pulse olives with sun dried tomatoes until mixture is uniform. Fold in garlic. Set aside.

9. Pipe phyllo with cheese mix, topped with 1/4 to 1/8 teaspoon of olive mix.

10. Garnish with basil.

SPICY EDAMAME HUMMUS

Serving Size: 8 - 10

6 tbsp rice wine vinegar
4 tbsp sugar
1 tsp kosher salt
3 c shelled edamame
1 c garbanzo beans
1 c garlic cloves, rough chop
1/2 c shallot, rough chop
2 ea small jalapeños, roasted and peeled
1/4 c tahini paste
1 ea lemon, juiced
TT kosher salt
soybean oil for poaching
1 c of ice cubes

1. In a small sauce pan, combine first 3 ingredients. Cook on medium-low and stir until dissolved.

2. Right before it comes to a boil, take off the heat, set aside.

3. Combine edamame, garbanzo beans, garlic, and shallots in a medium sauce pan. Add oil to just cover the edamame.

4. Turn to medium hat and cook until beans, garlic, and shallots are soft and cooked through. Strain and reserve oil.

5. Puree edamame, garbanzos, jalapeños (with seeds), shallots, and garlic in a blender. Add seasoned rice wine vinegar and a few ice cubes to keep the sauce from breaking.

6. Slowly stream in oil, a little at a time, until a smooth dip has formed. Stir in tahini and lemon juice.

7. Taste, season and adjust with salt. Chill in refrigerator until ready to serve.

8. Serve with crackers, bread, or veggies.

BRUSCHETTA

Serving Size: 6 - 8

I ordered this in an Italian restaurant where I was told by an Italian waiter that the correct pronunciation is [bru'sketta]. I quickly reminded him that we're in America and my wine glass was looking sad. We all learned something that day. Like how easy would this be to prepare at home? A large bowl, a baguette, veggies and oil...this is shit I keep in my house. Look out world, I'm getting cultured! *BRUSKETTA!*

- **2** tomatoes
- **1** tsp basil
- **2** tbsp olive oil
- **4** tbsp parmesan
- **1** tsp balsamic vinegar
- **1** tsp diced garlic
- **1** tsp kosher salt
- **1** baguette sliced
  black pepper TT

1. Preheat oven to 350 °F.

2. Combine all the ingredients in a large mixing bowl.

3. Spoon proportionate amount on each slice of baguette.

4. Bake in oven at 350°or 5 minutes or until cheese is melted.

BLOODY MARY SHRIMP COCKTAIL

Serving Size: 2 - 4

- **1** lb EZ peel shrimp, de-frosted & de-veined
- **2** ea lemons, halved
- **2 1/2** qt water
- **1/4** c kosher salt
- **2** ea avocado, diced
- **2** ea stalks of celery, julienned
  cilantro for garnish
  ### *BLOODY MARY COCKTAIL SAUCE*
- **1** c ketchup
- **1** tbsp horseradish
- **1** tsp garlic, minced
- **2** tsp Worcestershire
- **1** tsp Tabasco sauce
- **1** tsp celery salt
- **1/2** ea lemon, juiced
- **2** tbsp vodka

1. In a stockpot, add water, lemons, and salt.

2. Bring to a boil.

3. Add shrimp and cut off heat. Stir and cook until pink in color.

4. Shock in ice bath, peel and keep cool in the refrigerator.

5. For the sauce, combine all ingredients and chill.

6. Fill a serving glass with a little pool of bloody mary sauce. Top with avocado. Hang shrimps, tails facing out, on the rim of the glass. Place celery sticks between the shrimps. Garnish with a few sprigs of cilantro.

DEVILED EGGS

Serving Size: 12

You little devil, you. We know exactly what you're thinking. And the answer is, yes.. Deviled eggs can be topped with just about anything. (Oh Lord, here come the white people with the mayonnaise) In this case you'll find bacon, avocado, and diced olives to name a few. But be creative as you like. And in case that's not what you were thinking, let me have another go at it. And the answer is no. Our model Cam has never even seen a carb. Enjoy bitches!

12 eggs
1/2 c of mayonnaise
2 tsp yellow mustard
2 tsp white vinegar
1/4 tsp salt
TT Paprika
fresh ground black pepper

1. Put eggs in sauce pan with enough water to submerge eggs at least 2 inches.

2. Bring water to a boil for 2 minutes.

3. Reduce heat to low and cover sauce pan.

4. Continue to cook for 15 minutes.

5. Once cooked let cool and rinse in cool water.

6. Crack eggs, peel, and rinse thoroughly.

7. Cut eggs in half and remove yolks.

8. Put yolks into bowl and mash.

9. Place sliced eggs whites on serving dish.

10. Add mayo, mustard, vinegar, salt and pepper and mix.

11. Spoon mixture evenly into egg whites.

12. Add paprika and a dash of cayenne pepper for a bit of spice.

13. Sprinkle bits of cooked bacon and small diced pieces of avocado or green onion for extra flavor.

SPINACH ARTICHOKE DIP

Serving Size: 10 - 12

There are some cute tongue in cheek references in this book. So when I suggested this dish should be titled Spinach "Arti-Choke on my Dick!" you might be surprised to hear that the team thought it was a bit much. I don't really care, I'm just gonna take the model and this creamy dip home. I told him we were just gonna "watch Netflix and chill" anyway.

2 (10 oz) bags fresh baby spinach, chopped
1 (14 oz) can artichoke hearts, drained and chopped
1 c parmesan cheese, grated
1 c italian blend cheese
1 ea lemon, zested and juiced
1 tsp crushed red pepper flakes
5 ea cloves of garlic, minced
1 c sour cream
1 (8 oz) pkg cream cheese, softened
1/3 c mayo
1 1/2 c panko
1 tsp fresh rosemary, finely chopped
1 tsp fresh thyme leaves, finely chopped
2 tsp fresh parsley leaves, finely chopped
1 tbsp parmesan cheese, grated
1/2 stick of butter, melted
TT kosher salt and black pepper
Bread or crackers for dipping

1. Preheat oven to 350°F.

2. Combine 1 c parmesan, Italian blend, sour cream, cream cheese, mayo, garlic, red pepper flakes, lemon juice and zest.

3. Fold in spinach and artichokes. Taste for seasoning.

4. Pour into a greased baking dish and bake for 15 minutes.

5. While dip is baking, combine panko, rosemary, thyme, parsley and melted butter.

6. Top dip with panko mix and bake until golden. Serve hot.

STUFFED SHROOMS

Serving Size: 6

Calm down slutty hippies, it's not what you think it means! Wait, you thought it was breadcrumbs, parmesan, cream cheese, and sausage stuffed in baby portobello mushroom caps baked to perfection. I gotta say, pretty trippy man. Now, how 'bout a shower before dinner?

2 packages of whole baby portabella mushrooms

1 package cream cheese

1 tablespoon whole milk

1/4 c parmesan grated

1/4 c fine bread crumbs
garlic, salt, and black pepperTT

2 tablespoons green onions chopped

1 lb ground sausage cooked, drained, and cooled

1. Combine all ingredients except mushrooms together and mix well.

2. Remove stem from mushrooms and spoon each cap until mushroom top is stuffed.

3. Place mushrooms on baking sheet to where they will not fall on their sides.

4. Bake at 350° for 12 minutes.

BACON WRAPPED CHICKEN BREAST

Serving Size: 12

6 chicken breasts
12 bacon strips
8 oz sour cream
1 package chipped beef
1 can cream of mushroom soup
1 tbsp AP flour
1/4 c water

1. Flatten chicken breast with mallet.

2. Roll up the flattened chicken breast with the chipped beef inside.

3. Wrap the rolled up chicken breast with two strips of bacon.

4. Secure with a toothpick.

5. Line the 6 wrapped breasts in a 9x13 baking dish.

6. Mix the soup, sour cream, water, and flour in a mixing bowl.

7. Once mixed pour over the chicken breasts in baking dish.

8. Bake at 275 degrees for 3 hours.

***9.** Cut into small pieces for guests to enjoy as hor d'oeuvres or serve whole as an entree.*

GINGER MANGO ENDIVE SPOONS

Serving Size: 4

VINAIGRETTE

- **1** ea large navel orange, zested on microplane
- **1/4** c fresh squeezed orange juice
- **3** tbsp rice wine vinegar
- **2** tsp ginger root, peeled and minced
- **1** tsp garlic, minced
- **2** tsp honey
- **1/4** tsp chili flakes
- **3/4** c canola oil
- TT kosher salt

SALAD

- **8** ea Belgian endive
- cilantro sprigs, for garnish
- **3** ea ripe mangoes
- **1/3** c Japanese panko breadcrumbs, toasted

1. Preheat oven to 350°F. Pour panko on a sheet tray in an even layer. Toast until lightly golden, about 3 to 5 minutes. Set aside to cool.

2. Meanwhile, zest 1 orange, and juice to yield 1/4 cup. In a bowl, whisk orange juice, zest, vinegar, ginger, garlic, honey, and chili flakes. Whisk in oil in a slow steady stream until vinaigrette comes together. Add a couple pinches of salt and taste for seasoning. *Alternatively, vinaigrette can be made in a food processor or blender.

3. Cut skin off mangoes using a small, sharp knife or a peeler. Cut alongside seed of mango and dice into 1/4 inch cubes. Fold gently into vinaigrette.

4. To make endive spoons, cut off root end of endives. Separate the leaves onto a platter.

5. Spoon about 1 tablespoon of mixture onto endive leaves. Drizzle remaining vinaigrette around the leaves. Sprinkle toasted panko over endive spoons and garnish with cilantro sprigs.

This is it. The moment you have been waiting for.
You have committed whole heartedly and now you're
jumping in with both feet. It's time to go All the Way.
But don't throw all precautions to the wind.
In this day and age you have to be safe.
Refer to WESLO'S HOME-O-EROTIC COOKBOOK
and trust this experience will be magical one for
everyone involved.

All the Way

CHICKEN ALFREDO

Serving Size: 4 - 6

Interesting stains on your couch. Were you eating alfredo, watching Absolutely Fabulous and got so excited cream just started flying everywhere? Because that's what happened on my couch too. But if you're in need of a new recipe, I got you covered. And if you're in need of a good upholstery cleaner, I got a guy.

1/2 dried linguine

2 tbsp canola oil

1 1/4 lbs chicken breasts or thighs, skinless and boneless, cut into 1 1/2" pieces

4 ea garlic cloves, minced

1/4 c dry white wine

4 c heavy cream

1/8 tsp cayenne pepper

1 lemon, zested on microplane

1 1/2 c finely grated parmesan

3 tbsp unsalted butter

1/4 c finely chopped parsley, for garnish

TT kosher salt and black pepper

1. Prepare linguine according to package directions. Cook to al dente. Set aside.

2. In a large, high sided sauté pan, heat to medium-high heat. Add canola oil and tilt pan to distribute oil evenly. Season chicken with salt and pepper. Sear chicken until browned on all sides. Remove and let drain on paper towel. Chicken will finish cooking in sauce.

3. While pan is still on, add garlic and cook until fragrant, about 30 seconds. Deglaze pan with white wine, making sure to scrape up any browned bits stuck to the pan. When wine is almost all evaporated, add heavy cream. Add a couple pinches of salt and a pinch of pepper. Bring to a boil then drop to a simmer for 20 minutes. Toss chicken back in and cook for another 10 mins. Sauce should be reduced by half and be able to coat the back of a spoon. Turn off heat.

4. Add cheese in batches to ensure a creamy sauce. Adding all the cheese at once will make the alfredo sauce grainy.

5. Stir in cayenne pepper and lemon zest. Stir in butter a tablespoon at a time. Taste and adjust seasoning.

6. Toss linguine in sauce and split amongst four plates, making sure each plate gets some chicken. Garnish with additional cheese and parsley. Top with fresh cracked pepper if desired.

NEW YORK STRIPPER STEAK

Serving Size: 4

That's all.

___

- **4** ea (12 oz) strip steaks, room temperature
- **4** tbsp oil
- **4** tbsp shallots, minced
- **2** tbsp garlic, minced
- **1** c brandy
- **2** ea sprigs of thyme
- **1/2** c beef stock
- **2** tbsp unsalted butter
- TT kosher salt and black pepper.

1. Preheat oven to 400°F.

2. In a large, stainless steel sauté pan on high heat, add oil. Swirl pan to distribute oil evenly.

3. Salt and pepper both sides of steaks. Sear for 2 minutes without moving the steak. Flip steaks and sear for another minute. Transfer to a baking sheet and into the oven for 7 to 8 minutes. Let the steaks rest with foil tented over steaks, but not enclosed.

4. While steaks rest, make brandy sauce in the same pan. Turn pan back on to medium heat. Sweat the shallots for 1 minute. Add garlic and cook until fragrant. Turn heat on high, but take pan off heat. Tilt pan and add brandy to create a little pool. While pan is still tilted, scoot pan back to heat. The flame should ignite the brandy. Set pan back to flat position on burner. Shake until flame goes out and alcohol is cooked off, about 10 to 15 seconds. Much of the liquid will have evaporated.

5. Add beef stock and reduce heat to medium high. Cook until sauce is thickened and coats the back of a spoon. Turn off heat and stir in butter, one piece at a time, adding the next piece only after the first is completely incorporated. Serve alongside steaks.

CAJUN PASTA

Serving Size: 6-8

The Big Easy — hey, just like you!
I love New Orleans. Southern Decadence, Hurricanes, (the drink), and oh Lord...the food! Give me a creamy pasta with seafood and andouille sausage and you will see the happiest bitch alive. One who may very well need a nap after. Mind if I crash?

3 lbs cooked linguine
18 jumbo shrimp, peeled, de-veined, tails on
2 c andouille sausage, sliced on a bias
1 lb cooked crawfish tails
1 stick unsalted butter
1 8 oz pkg crimini mushrooms, quartered
1 c yellow onion, diced
1/2 c green bell pepper, diced
1/2 c celery, diced
1 tsp chili flakes
1/2 c dry white wine
1 ea small lemon, juiced
2 15 oz cans diced tomatoes
1 c heavy cream
3 tbsp green onion, thinly sliced
1/2 stick unsalted butter, cut into chunks
TT kosher salt and black pepper

1. In a large sauté pan, over medium-high heat, melt 1 stick of butter. Season shrimp with salt and pepper and sauté 1 to 2 minutes per side. Remove from pan and set aside. Shrimp will finish cooking in the sauce.

2. While pan is still hot, add mushrooms and brown for 3 minutes. Add in onion, bell peppers and celery. Cook until veggies are soft and translucent. Toss in garlic and chili flakes and cook for additional 30 seconds.

3. Deglaze with wine and lemon juice, scraping up any browned bits stuck on the bottom of the pan. When wine is reduced by half, add tomatoes, crawfish, sausage and shrimp. Cook for another 5 minutes.

4. Add heavy cream, stirring constantly, and reduce until sauce thickens and coats the back of a spoon. Turn off heat and stir in 1/2 stick of butter, one chunk at a time, making sure each chunk is completely incorporated before adding the next.

5. Toss in linguine and serve in bowls. Top with green onions and grated parmesan, if desired.

BAKED ZITI

Serving Size: 4 - 6

1 lb penne pasta cooked
1 chopped onion
1 lb browned ground beef
52 oz spaghetti sauce
6 oz provolone cheese
1 1/2 c sour cream
6 oz mozzarella cheese
2 tbsp parmesan

1. Brown beef with salt and garlic powder to taste.

2. Just before meat is completely cooked add diced onion.

3. Add spaghetti sauce to browned beef and let simmer.

4. Preheat oven to 350 degrees.

5. Layer half pasta in meat sauce in a baking dish.

6. Add provolone and sour cream.

7. Layer other half of pasta and meat sauce with mozzarella and parmesan.

8. Bake 30 minutes.

GREEN CHILE CHICKEN ENCHILADAS

Serving Size: 6 - 8

SAUCE

- **1** lb tomatillos, husked, rinsed and chopped
- **1** ea jalapeño
- **1** ea yellow onion, quartered
- **2** ea garlic cloves
- **1** 8 oz can hatch green chiles
- **1 1/2** c chicken stock
- **1/2** bunch of fresh cilantro
- **2** ea limes, juiced
- TT kosher salt

FILLING

- **1** ea rotisserie chicken, de-boned and shredded
- **1** ea yellow onion, sliced
- **2** ea garlic cloves, minced
- **1/4** c all purpose flour
- **3** c chicken stock
- **2** c monterey jack cheese, shredded
- **1** pkg white corn tortillas
- **1/2** c canola oil, for heating tortillas

1. In a large sauté pan over medium heat, sauté onion until soft and caramelized.

2. Stir in garlic and cook for another 30 seconds. Sprinkle in flour, stirring constantly for 1 minute.

3. Add stock and turn heat to medium-high heat. Scrape up any browned bits stuck at the bottom of the pan.

4. Stir in 1 c of green chile sauce to pan, and cut off heat. Toss in chicken.

5. Add stock and turn heat to medium-high heat. Scrape up any browned bits stuck at the bottom of the pan.

6. Stir in 1 cup of green chile sauce to pan, and cut off heat. Toss in chicken.

ASSEMBLY

1. Preheat oven to 350°F.

2. In a large sauté pan on medium high heat, heat oil.

3. Using tongs, cook tortillas 10 seconds per side in oil.

4. Do not fry. Cool just long enough so that tortillas are pliable.

5. Fill each tortilla with some filling and a little cheese. Roll like a cigar and place in a greased baking dish, seam side down.

6. Repeat with remaining tortillas. Ladle green chile sauce over enchiladas and top with remaining cheese. Bake until cheese is melted and edges are slightly browned.

SPICY SALMON

Serving Size: 4

Looking to spice up your love life? Can't help you there. But if your dish needs a little kick, I got your back. Cayenne has always been my go to, and when added over a salmon filet with a bit of garlic, onion powder, and sea salt...hell, it could very well help your love life too. So there.
You're welcome.

2 1/2	pound salmon fillets
1	jar of alfredo cheese sauce
	cayenne pepper TT
1	package of tortellini
	sea salt
	unsalted butter

1. Place salmon on pan in 2 oz of water on medium low heat.

2. Cook both sides for 5 minutes each as water begins to evaporate.

3. Add sea salt to taste and 1/4 tsp of cayenne pepper.

4. Drain remaining water if any.

5. Add 2 tsp of olive oil to pan.

6. Grill both sides in oil for 30 seconds each.

7. Boil tortellini in medium saucepan with butter for 5 minutes.

8. Drain but not entirely. Leave a bit of moisture to avoid drying pasta.

9. Add an additional tsp of butter to pasta once you return to the pan and stir.

10. Plate tortellini and place salmon fillet on bed of pasta

11. Heat jar of alfredo in sauce pan at medium low heat until hot.

12. Add additional cayenne pepper for extra spice

13. Drizzle alfredo sauce over the top of fillet Garnish with parsley and serve

JAMAICAN JERK CHICKEN

Serving Size: 8

Mangoes, rum, reggae...and now the best way to marinade a bird. Jamaican me real hungry gurl. Like real, real hungry. This stupid amount of weed I smoked probably didn't hurt either.

---

8 ea chicken quarters
1/2 c white vinegar
3 tbsp dark rum
1/2 c fresh squeezed orange juice
2 tbsp fresh squeezed lime juice
1/4 c soy
2 tbsp brown sugar
4 ea cloves of garlic
1 tbsp fresh ginger root
2 ea scotch bonnets or habaneros
3 tbsp fresh thyme leaves
1 bunch green onion, roughly chopped
1 tbsp allspice
1 tsp cinnamon
1 pinch nutmeg
TT kosher salt and black pepper

1. Combine all ingredients, except the chicken, in a food processor. Marinate chicken in a zip top bag for 4 hours or overnight for intense heat.

2. Preheat grill to medium heat.

3. Remove chicken from marinade. Salt and pepper chicken, and grill for approximately 45 mins or until juices run clear and there is no more blood.

RIBEYE

Serving Size: 4

From man's rib God made Eve. From cow's rib He made rib eye. Coincidence? I think not! Although I might have detoured from where I was going with this, allow me to get back to the point. We're about to eat steak. Look like you belong here!

---

4 ea (8 to 10 oz) ribeyes 1" thick
1/2 c balsamic vinegar
1/4 c soy
1/2 tbsp crushed red pepper flakes
1 tbsp garlic, minced
1 tbsp shallots, minced
3 tbsp brown sugar
8 ea fresh thyme sprigs
TT kosher salt and black pepper

1. Combine the first 8 ingredients in a zip top bag. Marinate for 2 hours to overnight.

2. Let steaks sit out in room temp for 30 to 40 minutes.

3. Preheat grill on high. Season both sides with salt and pepper and grill for 4 to 5 minutes per side for medium rare.

SPAGHETTI & MEATBALLS

Serving Size: 4

This might normally be a really basic bitch recipe for you, but not today. Oh no! Today we're gonna make a few changes. Why? Because friends don't let friends eat wet noodles and ketchup! That's why. And at this point we're kinda like besties. Right? Right?! Cool. In this recipe you'll get the full experience and flavor that only comes using fresh ingredients. Guaranteed to leave such a thick aroma, your neighbors will hate you. Do you feel Italian already? Me too!

---

1 1/2 spaghetti, cooked
1 ea onion, small diced
2 tbsp garlic, minced
1 1/2 lbs ground beef
1 1/2 lbs ground pork
1 egg, beaten
1 c milk
4 ea slices of white bread, crust removed
1/2 tbsp chili flakes
1/2 c grated parmesan
1 tbsp honey
3 tbsp fresh basil leaves, chiffonade
1 tbsp fresh oregano leaves, chopped
1 tbsp fresh thyme leaves, chopped
TT kosher salt and black pepper
2 ea jar of favorite pasta sauce

1. Preheat oven to 350°F.

2. Cook pasta according to package instructions. Set aside.

3. In a medium bowl, tear bread into pieces and pour milk over. Set aside to soak.

4. Combine meats, salt, pepper, chili flakes, parmesan, herbs, honey, and bread mixture. Mix until combined. Do not over mix or meatballs will be tough.

5. Lightly roll meatballs into golf ball size balls, and bake on a cookie sheet or mini muffin pan for 15 to 20 mins or until browned.

6. While meatballs are cooking, heat up pasta sauce on medium heat until heated through.

7. When meatballs are browned, add meatballs to sauce and simmer for 15 mins. Serve over spaghetti and top with parmesan cheese if desired.

BABY BACK RIBS

Serving Size: 6 - 8

You know it's good when you're not afraid to get it all over you. Steal the show with delicious Southern inspired recipe. You'll be sure to take home the crown home.

- **2** ea racks of baby back ribs
- **1/2** c brown sugar, packed
- **2** tsp chili powder
- **1** tbsp paprika
- **2** tsp cayenne
- **2** tsp garlic powder
- **2** tsp onion powder
- **1** tbsp fresh thyme
  TT kosher salt and black pepper

1. Wash ribs under cold water and remove membrane from underside. Pat dry.

2. Combine the next 7 ingredients.

3. Salt and pepper both sides. Generously season all around with dry rub mix. Wrap in double layer of foil and marinate overnight in the refrigerator.

4. Allow ribs to sit out at room temperature for 1 hour.

5. Bake in a 300°F for 2 hours. Remove from oven and let cool for 30 minutes.

6. Brush on any BBQ sauce thinned with some of the drippings and grill or broil for 5 minutes or until a nice crust forms.

MEAT LOAF

Serving Size: 4 - 6

1 1/2	pounds of ground beef or ground turkey
1	red bell pepper
1	yellow or green bell pepper
5	garlic cloves mashed
1/2	tsp red pepper flakes
1	egg
1	c panko or bread crumbs
1/2	c parmesan
1/2	c ketchup
2	tbsp balsamic vinegar

1. Sauté vegetables in olive oil until almost tender.

2. Whisk egg in a separate bowl.

3. Add panko, cheese, ketchup, balsamic vinegar, and all sautéd veggies into bowl with and mix thoroughly.

4. Add beef into mixture and mash until beef is completely wet.

5. Put mixed beef into a loaf pan and bake at 425°F for 1 hour.

GLAZED STUFFED PORK CHOPS

Serving Size: 6

STUFFING

- **1** large white onion diced
- **2** boxes of Stove Top Seasoned Bread
- **1** apple diced
- **3** stalks of celery diced
- **1/2** c of butter
  heavy cream

---

1. Sauté the onion, apple and celery in butter.

2. Add seasoned bread pieces.

3. Add heavy cream slowly to reach desired moisture.

PORK CHOPS

- **6** pork chops
- **2** granny smith apples
- **1/3** c vinaigrette (balsamic, raspberry, or cranberry)
- **1** tbsp brown sugar
- **1** tbsp dijon mustard
  salt and pepper TT

1. Mix the vinaigrette and brown sugar and dijon mustard and set aside.

2. Slice pork chops almost to a butterfly to make a pocket.

3. Stuff pork chops with prepared dressing.

4. All the remaining stuffing can be put into the bottom of a 9x13 baking dish.

5. Season the stuffed with salt and pepper and brown in a separate frying pan.

6. Take the browned pork chops and lay them over the stuffing in the baking dish.

7. Place two apple rings or thin slices on top of the pork chops and brush with the vinaigrette.

8. Bake at 375 degrees for 25 minutes.

9. Plate and drizzle individually with vinaigrette mixture,

THE wHOLE ENCHILADA

Serving Size: 6

When it gets so hot and you have to have it all, you can only be talking about one thing. You want the wHole Enchilada. Luckily for you and your guests we have a recipe that will make everyone feel like they got more than their share. Bet you can't fit the whole thing in your mouth. But seriously don't try that. You'll just choke and try to sue me. And I just hate that.

1	lb ground beef
12	corn tortillas
1	can red enchilada sauce
1	small onion diced
1	shredded monterey jack cheese
2/3	c cheese crumbles
1/2	tsp garlic powder
1/2	tsp onion powder
	sea salt TT
	vegetable oil
	diced pickled jalapeños

1. Brown beef and season with garlic powder, onion powder and sea salt.

2. Just before beef is ready add half cup of onions.

3. Save other half of onions for later Heat pan with 2 tbsp of vegetable oil at medium heat.

4. Grill tortillas for 45 seconds on each side and place on plate with a napkin to absorb oil.

You will have to add more oil as you need it

ASSEMBLY

1. Once tortillas are all grilled add a spoonful of ground beef and a pinch of crumbled cheese.

2. Lay each rolled tortilla in a baking pan side by side in a neat row.

3. Spoon out desired amount of enchilada sauce over each rolled tortilla.

4. Pour shredded cheese over dish.

5. Pour extra onions and diced jalapeños over dish.

6. Bake at 425° for 10 minutes.

7. Serve piping hot!

GINGER GLAZED SALMON

Serving Size: 4

This recipe may take a while, so get comfortable. And if I'm spending all day cooking for you, just know I'll be expecting something in return. I'm putting my everything into this dish. So what I'm expecting is for you is to eat all of me. Every last bite. Now get out of my kitchen and go watch your Drag Race.

4 ea (5-6 oz) salmon filets
1/2 c brown sugar, packed
1/4 c honey
1/2 c soy sauce
1/2 tsp crushed pepper flakes
1 tsp ginger root, rough chopped
4 ea garlic cloves, smashed
3 ea green onions, white part only, rough chopped
8 ea cilantro stems
1 ea orange

1. Using a peeler, remove zest from orange.

2. Juice orange and place both zest and juice in a large saucepan.

3. Add brown sugar, honey, soy, red pepper, ginger, garlic, cilantro stems to saucepan.

4. Bring to a boil and drop to simmer for 10-12 minutes or until sauce coats the back of a spoon.

5. Strain and cool. Brush sauce over salmon and allow to marinate at room temperature for 15-30 minutes.

6. Bake in a 400°F oven for 4 minutes.

7. Baste with glaze and cook for 4 more minutes.

8. Before serving, brush with one more coat of glaze.

9. Garnish with toasted sesame seeds if desired.

10. Serve hot.

ZESTY GRILLED CHICKEN

Serving Size: 6 - 8

Chicken, the perfect protein. Well, one of them. Prepared right it can help keep off the unwanted pounds, and with the right seasoning it won't taste like that's what it's doing. This dish is going to make your taste buds run wild without any of the guilt. We'll save the guilt for dessert.

---

4 lbs skinless, boneless chicken
2 c greek yogurt
1 1/2 tsp crushed red pepper flakes
2 tbsp shallot, minced
1 tbsp garlic, minced
2 ea lemons, zested
1/4 tsp turmeric
1 tbsp paprika
1 tsp cumin
1/2 tsp ginger
1/4 tsp cinnamon
TT kosher salt and black pepper

1. Combine all ingredients in a zip top bag and marinate overnight.

2. Preheat grill and let chicken sit out in room temperature for 30 minutes.

3. Salt and pepper chicken and grill over medium heat on a greased grill grate.

4. The marinade should form a crust while it cooks. Chicken is done when juices run clear and chicken registers at 165°F.

The urge to stray away from your main love can be a temptation we all face. I mean how easy it to lose focus with creamy Gouda Mac n Cheese staring at you from the other side of your plate? It's just begging you to indulge in it's pleasures. It's ok gurl.. No one here will judge. Just don't look so guilty when you return to your main dish.

On the Side

GOUDA MAC N CHEESE

Serving Size: 6

Oh carbs, you whore! Don't you look at me like that. You know I'm weak. And if I'm gonna keep feeling like a lady, I need to play hard to get for at least ten more minutes. Who am I kidding? I knew you were gonna be here, that's the only reason I came. I know I'll probably just miss you as soon as your gone but one thing is certain - It's gonna be a Gouda time.

6 individual ceramic ramekins, buttered
1 lb dried elbow macaroni
2 1/2 c milk
2 tbsp unsalted butter, plus 1 tbsp for buttering ramekins
2 tbsp all purpose flour
1/2 ea small yellow onion, small dice
2 sprigs of thyme
1 ea bay leaf
6 ea peppercorn
4 ea parsley, stems only
1/4 tsp cayenne pepper
4 oz smoked gouda
1 ea small lemon, zested and juiced
1 c Japanese panko
3 tbsp butter, melted
2 tbsp parsley, finely chopped

1. Preheat oven to 375°F. Take 1 tablespoon and butter ramekins. Set aside.

2. Cook macaroni according to directions on package.

3. In a small saucepan, heat milk with onion, thyme, bay, peppercorns and parsley stems on medium heat. Strain and reserve.

4. In a medium saucepan, melt 2 tablespoons of butter on medium high heat. When butter is melted, add flour and whisk. Cook until raw flour smell subsides and roux takes on nutty note, about 2 minutes. Whisk in milk and cook until sauce thickens and coats the back of a spoon. Season with salt and pepper, cayenne, and lemon juice. Remove from heat.

5. While sauce is still hot, sprinkle in Gouda in small batches. (Adding cheese in all at once will result in a grainy sauce.) Fold in macaroni.

6. In a small bowl, combine panko, lemon zest, parsley, and melted butter.

7. Fill ramekins with mac and top with panko mixture. Bake until golden, about 8 to 10 minutes.

POTATO SALAD

Serving Size: 10 - 12

Potato Salad is a lot like a Britney remix. No one is ever all that excited about it - but done right it can be a big hit. In this case we'll have your guests asking you to hit them one more time for seconds. Think that joke was cheesy? Wait for the next recipe.

---

5 lbs baby yukon potatoes, rinsed & scrubbed
6 ea eggs
1 lb bacon, cut into lardons
1 ea yellow onion, small dice
1 c mayo
1 c sour cream
1 tbsp whole grain mustard
3 ea celery, small dice
   TT kosher salt and black pepper

1. In a large pot, bring water to a boil. Add potatoes and cook until small knife inserted shows no resistance but potatoes should not be falling apart, 15 to 20 minutes.

2. Place eggs in a small sauce pan. Cover with cold water. Bring to a boil, then turn off. Cover and let sit for 12 minutes. Shock in ice bath and peel. Chop and set aside.

3. While potatoes and eggs are working, place lardons in an even layer on a cold, large sauté pan. Turn on to medium heat, and let the fat render out. When the bacon is crispy, remove with a slotted spoon to a plate lined with paper towels. Add onions to the hot bacon fat and cook until caramelized.

4. By now the potatoes should be done. Drain potatoes and quarter. Sprinkle with salt and pepper and return to colander. Pour caramelized onions with bacon fat over potatoes. The bacon fat will flavor the potatoes further and the excess fat will drain through. Give the potatoes a nice shake to remove remaining fat and transfer to a large bowl.

5. Mix together mayo, sour cream and mustard. Fold into potatoes along with celery, eggs and green onions. Taste and adjust seasonings. Chill for 1 to 2 hours.

SCALLOPED POTATOES WITH HAM

Serving Size: 6 - 8

Hallelujah! It's Raining Cheese! And bitch, I love Cheddar. You might even say it's my spirit animal. But melted and gooey, baked over potatoes and diced ham. You didn't have to do all that. But you did. So thank you.

4 c milk

1 ea yellow onion, rough chop

4 ea sprigs of thyme

1 ea bay leaf

6 ea black peppercorns

4 ea parsley, stems only

4 tbsp unsalted butter

4 tbsp AP flour

pinch nutmeg

2 tsp garlic powder

1/8 tsp cayenne

1 tbsp dijon mustard

2 1/2 c grated sharp cheddar

1 1/2 lb diced ham

3 lbs russets, rinsed and scrubbed

1. Preheat oven to 350°F.

2. In a small saucepan, heat milk with onion, thyme, bay, peppercorns and parsley stems on medium heat just until it steams. Do not boil. Strain and reserve.

3. In a medium saucepan, melt butter on medium high heat. When butter is melted, add flour and whisk. Cook until raw flour smell subsides and roux takes on nutty note, about 2 minutes. Whisk in milk and cook until sauce thickens and coats the back of a spoon. Season with salt and pepper, garlic powder, nutmeg and cayenne. Remove from heat.

4. While sauce is still hot, sprinkle in 2 of cheddar in small batches. (Adding cheese in all at once will result in a grainy sauce.)

5. On a mandolin, slice potatoes, skin on, to 1/8" thickness. Working in batches so that potatoes do not oxidize and turn brown, layer a buttered baking dish with potatoes, ham, and sauce. Slice more potatoes and repeat. After the last layer of sauce is added, top with remaining 1/2 cup of cheddar. Bake 35 to 40 minutes.

ROASTED ASSPARAGUS

Serving Size: 6

I heard these make your pee stink... or burn. I can't remember. While I slept through most of health class, I do know that when I bake these little guys in olive oil, a little salt and pepper, then top with parm, it could very well make my dick fall off. I'd still eat them. Just kidding. No one loves my dick more than me.

- **2** bunches large asparagus
- **2** tbsp olive oil
- TT kosher salt
- TT black pepper
- **1/2** c parmesan cheese finely grated or microplaned

1. Cut woodsy ends of asparagus off, about 1" from the bottom.

2. Using a peeler, shave off the outer part of asparagus, about 1 1 1/2" from bottom.

3. Lay asparagus in a sheet pan, drizzle with olive oil and toss with salt and pepper.

4. Roast in oven until tender but still crisp, about 10 to 12 minutes.

5. Remove asparagus from oven and toss with parmesan while still hot. Serve immediately.

GARLIC CHEDDAR MASHED POTATOES

Serving Size: 4 - 6

Hey daddy! Wanna smash papas? Me too! But just so you know, I'm now expecting you to buy me drinks all night and hear about how I walked in a friend's runway show. Just kidding... God! You're easier than my ex. What I do expect though, is for you to be floored once you bite into the divinity that is creamy garlic flavored potatoes with aged white cheddar. Hey, some things just get better with age. I'm just gonna keep telling myself that.

4	ea russet potatoes, peeled and cut into 1" cubes
1	ea whole bulb of garlic
1	tbsp olive oil
1/2	c whole milk
1/4	c heavy cream
1/4	c (1/2 stick) unsalted butter, room temperature
8	oz grated white cheddar
	TT kosher salt and black pepper
3	tbsp chives, thinly chopped (for garnish)

1. Preheat oven to 400°F. Cut the top end off bulb of garlic. drizzle with olive oil and wrap in foil. Bake for 30 to 35 minutes or until garlic is soft and light brown in color.

2. While garlic is roasting, place cubed potatoes in a large pot. Cover with cold water and turn on to high heat. Bring to a boil, then drop down to a simmer until potatoes are cooked through, about 20 minutes.

3. Pull out garlic and let cool for 5 minutes before squeezing cloves out. Set roasted cloves aside and discard empty bulb.

4. In a small saucepan, heat cream and milk on medium heat until steams. Do not boil. Cut off heat.

5. Drain potatoes. Return potatoes to pot and turn heat back on to low. Heat until all excess water has evaporated from potatoes and steam dissipates. With a potato masher, combine butter and roasted garlic into potatoes. Add a generous amount of salt and a few pinches of black pepper.

6. Fold in half milk/cream mixture until combined. Fold in more milk/cream mixture into potatoes until light and fluffy. Fold in cheddar. Taste and adjust seasonings. Serve and top with chives.

ITALIAN PASTA SALAD

Serving Size: 4 - 6

Sports car? Cool. Italian Sports Car? Fuck me daddy!
Works the same with pasta salad, trust.

---

2 lbs favorite pasta
1/3 c balsamic vinegar
1 ea orange, zested and juiced
1 ea small shallot, minced
3 ea clove of garlic, minced
1 tsp dijon mustard
1 tbsp honey
2/3 c olive oil
1 ea container of bocconcini mozzarella
3 ea baby cucumbers, sliced
1 pt cherry tomatoes, halved
1 ea small red onion, thinly sliced
1 c fresh basil
TT kosher salt and black pepper

1. Cook pasta according to package for *al dente* pasta.

2. While pasta cooks, combine the next 6 ingredients in a blender on medium speed. Turn the speed to high and slowly drizzle in the olive oil until emulsified. Add salt and pepper, taste and adjust. Set aside.

3. Drain the pasta and let cool slightly. Transfer to serving bowl. Toss warm pasta with dressing. Add cucumbers, tomatoes, and onion. Taste and adjust seasoning with more salt and pepper if needed. Chill for at least 2 hours. Can be made the day before.

4. Right before serving, fold in bocconcini and basil chiffonade.

GREEN BEAN CASSEROLE

Serving Size: 6 - 8

Green beans are so healthy. At least they were. Then we added heavy cream, fried onions and sherry wine. I know, I just love makeovers. Strut your stuff, green beans. You're officially a fierce bitch! And I'm officially a fat bitch. **#StillSexyTho**

---

1 (16 oz) pkg white button mushrooms, sliced thin
4 tbsp vegetable oil
6 ea sprigs thyme
1/2 c yellow onion, small diced
2 tbsp garlic, minced
1/4 c sherry wine
1/4 c AP flour
1 c chicken stock
2 c heavy cream
1/4 tsp cayenne
1 ea lemon, zested and juiced
2 lbs haricot verts, cleaned and blanched
1 ea can fried onions
TT kosher salt and black pepper

1. Preheat oven to 400°F.

2. In a large sauté pan on medium high, heat oil until just smoking. Add mushrooms in an even layer, stirring occasionally until mushroom have taken a little color. Add onions, thyme, salt and pepper. Cook until onions are translucent. Add garlic and cook until fragrant. Deglaze with sherry until liquid is almost gone. Discard thyme.

3. Add flour and stir for another 2 minutes. Pour in chicken stock, cream, and cayenne. Reduce until sauce coats the back of a spoon. Remove from heat. Add lemon zest and juice.

4. Toss in haricot verts and 1/4 of the fried onions. Pour into a buttered baking dish and top with remaining fried onions. Bake for 15 minutes until bubbly. Serve hot.

In this chapter we explore the climactic experience that is
A Sweet Finish. If we're being perfectly honest,
it's probably why you came in the first place.

These sweet little bits of heaven will leave you trembling
and begging for more, so keep a napkin handy.

A Sweet Finish

RAINBOW COOKIES

Serving Size: 6 - 8

Don't half ass anything. Use your whole ass! So when making cookies I encourage you to be as festive as that jacket I discouraged you from buying. Making a multitude of patterns gives your guests the illusion of option. Your place or mine?

---

2 1/2 c AP flour
1 tsp baking soda
1 tsp cream of tartar
1/4 tsp salt
2 sticks unsalted butter, softened
1 c sugar
1 ea egg, room temperature
1 ea vanilla bean, scraped
1 ea lemon, zested

1. Sift together dry ingredients.

2. In a mixer with a paddle attachment, cream together butter and sugar. Add eggs, vanilla, and lemon zest.

3. Slowly add in dry ingredients. Scraped down sides and make sure all flour in incorporated. Place dough between two large sheets of wax paper and roll to 1/4" thickness. Chill for 1 hour.

4. Preheat oven to 375°F.

5. Remove dough from fridge. Using any kind of cookie cutter, cut out cookies and place on a lined cookie sheet. Pop in freezer for 10 minutes. Chilling the cutouts before baking will keep the shape of the cookie. Bake for 8 minutes until cookies show very light golden color on edges. Do not bake further or cookie will come out dry and crumbly.

6. When cooled, decorate cookies with different colored royal icing to create your rainbow cookies.

ANGEL FOOD CAKE

Serving Size: 4 - 6

Did it hurt your ass when you fell from heaven? Hoping not, sweet cheeks. But if it did, come sit next to me for a piece of Angel Food Cakes. I love these. Not a lot of sugar and you can top these cakes with practically any fruit. Heaven awaits!

1	c cake flour
1 3/4	c caster sugar (superfine sugar)
1/4	tsp salt
12	ea large egg whites, room temperature
1 1/2	tsp cream of tartar
1	ea vanilla bean, scraped
2	tbsp amaretto
1	ea small orange, zested
1	ea small lemon, zested

1. Preheat oven to 350°F.

2. Sift flour, salt, and half of the sugar. Set aside.

3. Whisk egg whites, amaretto, and cream of tartar until foamy. With a hand mixer on medium speed, stream remaining sugar in slowly until soft peaks form.

4. Add vanilla, orange and lemon zest. Mix until stiff peaks and glossy. Do not over beat.

5. Fold dry mix into meringue in batches. With each addition, batter should look shaggy and be streaked with flour still before adding next batch of flour. Over mixing will cause meringue to deflate.

6. Scoop batter into an ungreased tube pan. The inner tube allows the batter to climb, creating a light and fluffy cake.

7. Bake for 35 to 40 minutes, making sure not open the oven before the first 35 minutes. A toothpick inserted should come out clean and cake should spring back when surface is lightly pressed.

BOTTOMS UP PINEAPPLE CAKE

Serving Size: 8 - 10

What a Bottom! Even your cake is bottoms up. Sorry, I couldn't help myself.
This yummy cake is baked with pineapple juice and whole slices. Maraschino cherries add an extra bit of zing and some much needed color. Sweet and juicy. Just like me.

1	(20oz) can of pineapple slices, drained
6-8	maraschino cherries, halved
4	tbsp unsalted butter
1/2	c light brown sugar
1	tbsp dark rum
3	ea egg yolks
3/4	c sugar
1/2	c sour cream
1 1/2	c cake flour
3/4	tsp baking powder
1/4	tsp baking soda
1/4	tsp salt
1	stick + 1 tbsp unsalted butter, softened
1/4	c pineapple puree

1. Preheat oven to 350°F.

2. Drain pineapple slices and dry with paper towels.

3. This cake is best made in a cast iron pan to create a nice caramelized crust, but can alternately be made in a greased baking pan.

4. Melt butter in pan on medium heat. Stir in brown sugar and rum until moistened. Cut off heat. If using a cast iron, arrange pineapple slices straight into bottom of the pan, using half slices for the sides of the pan. In the center of each pineapple, place a maraschino, cut side up.

5. Pulse remaining pineapple slices in a food processor to yield 1/4 cup of purée. In a bowl, whisk egg yolks and sugar until pale and doubled in size. Stir in sour cream. In a separate bowl, sift flour, baking powder, baking soda, and salt.

6. Using a mixer, cream together butter and sugar until light and fluffy. Add flour mix alternately with yolk mix to the mixer, starting and ending with the flour mix.

7. Fold in pineapple puree.

8. Pour batter into prepared pan and bake in the center of the oven for 45 minutes or until toothpick inserted comes out clean. Cool slightly and run a small knife around the edge of the pan before flipping over. Serve warm.

COCONUT CREAMPIE

Serving Size: 6 - 8

If you're banging a coconut to completion, you're doing it wrong. If you're using toasted coconut, fresh milk, and vanilla, you're well on your way to having yourself a yummy slice the whole table will love. Now wash up and try again.

PIE CRUST

1 1/2	c AP flour
1	tbsp sugar
1/2	tsp salt
6	tbsp unsalted butter, cold
1/4	c ice water

FILLING

1 1/2	c coconut milk
1 1/2	c heavy cream
1/2	tsp salt
1/2	tsp vanilla extract
2	ea eggs
1	ea egg yolk
1/2	c sugar
1/4	c cornstarch
2	tbsp butter
1	c sweetened coconut flakes

TOPPING

1	(14oz) can coconut cream or full fat coconut milk chilled overnight
1/2	c confectioners sugar

---

1. Blend flour, sugar and salt in a food processor. Add cold butter and pulse until mixture resembles coarse meal. Drizzle 4 tbsp of ice water over mixture. Process just until moist clumps form, adding more water if dough is dry. Gather dough into a ball, flatten into a disk, and wrap in plastic. Chill for 1 hour.

2. Roll out dough between 2 sheets of plastic or wax paper. Roll out into 14" round. Transfer to 9" pie dish. Crimp edges, pierce all over bottom and sides with a fork. Freeze for 15 minutes.

3. Preheat oven to 375°F.

4. Line crust with aluminum foil and fill with pie weights, dried beans or uncooked rice.

5. Bake for 20 minutes. Remove weights and foil, bake until golden. Let cool before filling.

6. For the filling, combine coconut milk, heavy cream, and salt into a saucepan. Heat until mixture begins to steam. Remove from heat.

7. In a bowl, whisk eggs, egg yolk, sugar, and cornstarch. Ladle hot milk into eggs, whisking to not curdle eggs. Pour egg mix into remaining milk and turn heat to medium. Using a rubber spatula, cook mixture slowly until thickened to pudding consistency. Add vanilla extract. Remove from heat, cool slightly, and add butter, one tbsp at a time until completely incorporated. Stir in coconut flakes.

8. Pour custard into pie crust and chill for 3 hours or overnight.

9. When ready to serve, remove coconut cream or milk from fridge without shaking. Scrape out the thickened cream on top, leaving the liquid behind.

10. Use a hand mixer to beat the cream and powdered sugar until creamy and smooth. Top pie and serve.

BANANA PUDDING

Serving Size: 4

Is that a banana in your pudding or are you happy to see me? Why can't it be both? With this recipe it can be, and so much more! This batch of joy is mixed with banana liqueur, topped with homemade whipped cream, and layered with vanilla wafers. Preparing this yummy treat is sure to make everyone happy to see you!

---

5 ea egg yolks
1/2 c granulated sugar
1/4 c cornstarch
   pinch kosher salt
2 c milk
1 ea vanilla bean, halved and scraped
3 tbsp banana liqueur
2 tbsp unsalted butter, cut into chunks, chilled
3 ea ripe bananas
1 ea lemon juiced
1/2 box vanilla wafers
1/2 c heavy cream
3 tbsp granulated sugar

---

1. Preheat oven to 325°F. Toast wafers on a cookie sheet for 5 to 8 minutes. Let cool.

2. In a mixing bowl, whisk yolks and sugar until pale in color and doubled in size. Whisk in cornstarch.

3. In a medium saucepan over medium heat, combine milk, vanilla bean, seeds and pod halves, and a pinch of salt. Heat until milk steams. Do not boil.

4. Quickly whisk in one ladle of hot milk mixture to yolk mixture, pouring the milk in one slow, steady stream. Pour remaining milk mixture into yolk mixture. Whisk until combined.

5. Return mixture to saucepan. Using a rubber spatula, cook pudding slowly until thickened. Remove from heat.

6. Discard vanilla pod halves, and add banana liqueur.

7. Chip in cold butter into pudding, stirring continuously until all butter is incorporated. Transfer to a bowl, and lay a piece of plastic on the surface of the pudding so a skin does not form. Chill for 2 to 3 hours.

8. While pudding is chilling, whisk together heavy cream and 3 Tbsp sugar. Whisk until soft peaks form. Cover and chill.

9. After 3 hours, remove plastic wrap from pudding. Give the pudding a quick whisk, then using a rubber spatula, fold in the whip cream until combined.

10. Cut bananas into 1/4 inch rounds and toss in lemon juice to prevent browning. Fold into pudding.

11. To assemble, use any decorative glass. It could be fancy martini glasses or cute little mason jars. Place a dollop of pudding at the bottom of the glass.

12. Add a layer of toasted wafers, and keep alternating, ending with a layer of pudding. Finish the tops with crushed wafers and cover. Chill overnight.

C R E A M   P U F F S

Serving Size: 18 - 20

Remember when Twinkies almost went extinct? Not those kind of Twinkies – there's no shortage there. The packaged ones with the everlasting shelf life. In case you're not one to stock up, I recommend learning to make these sweet little numbers. Best when fresh. Hey, just like the other kind of Twinkies.

---

1 stick unsalted butter
1 c water
1 tbsp sugar
1/2 tsp salt
1 c AP flour
3 ea eggs

FILLING

2 c milk
1 ea vanilla bean, scraped
4 ea egg yolks
1/2 c sugar
1/8 tsp salt
1/2 c heavy cream

---

1. Begin with the filling. Bring milk, 1/4 c sugar, vanilla bean to a simmer. Remove from heat.

2. Whisk egg yolks, remaining sugar, and salt in a bowl. Slowly add cornstarch and combine.

3. Ladle hot milk mixture into eggs, whisking to prevent eggs from curdling. Return mixture back into saucepan and cook over medium heat until thick. Transfer to a bowl and lay plastic wrap directly onto surface of custard. Chill for an hour.

4. Beat heavy cream until soft peaks and set in fridge.

5. While the filling is chilling, make dough for cream puffs.

6. Preheat oven to 425°F.

7. In a large saucepan, bring water, butter, salt and sugar to a boil. Add all flour at once and turn down to low. Use a wooden spoon to stir and incorporate all flour.

8. Cook off and on heat until some moisture has evaporated and some dough begins to stick to the bottom of the pan. Transfer to a stand mixer with paddle attachment.

9. Turn mixer on medium speed. Add eggs one at a time, making sure each egg is incorporated and bottom and sides of mixer are scraped down before adding the next egg. Transfer to a pastry bag fitted with a large plain tip.

10. Pipe 2" balls onto a lined baking sheet 1" apart. Use a wet finger to push down any tips that may burn during baking. Bake for 15 minutes, then reduce the oven to 375°F until puffed up and light golden brown. Avoid opening the oven while baking. Remove from oven and pierce to release steam. Let cool on baking sheet.

11. Remove custard and whip cream from fridge. Whisk half the whip cream with the custard, and fold in remaining whip cream. Pipe into cream puffs and chill until ready to serve, not to exceed 4 hours in fridge.

GINGER BEARS

Serving Size: 6

Ginger and a bear? It must be Christmas and here's the perfect recipe for the holiday season! Warm, lightly sweetened, and fun to decorate. Use small dry fruits like raisins, cranberries, or even chocolate chips for features like a nose and eyes. You can also use icing to draw lines and shapes.
It's like build-a-bear boyfriend edition. Cute and sad all at the same time. Now try not to kill yourself over the holidays. Ain't nobody got time for that!

---

1 1/2 c butter

2 c sugar

2 Eggs

1/3 c molasses

4 1/2 c flour

2 tsp baking soda

1 tsp salt

1 tsp ginger

2 tsp cinnamon

1. Beat together and roll out.

2. Cut into Bear Shapes with a cookie cutter or do like us and build your own.

3. Bake at 375°F for 8 minutes.

4. Remove Bears from oven and while your bears are still soft add raisins, dried cranberries, or chocolate chips for eyes, nose, and belly button.

OATMEAL RAISIN COOKIES

Serving Size: 12

- **1** c white sugar
- **1** c raisins
- **1** c butter
- **2** eggs
- **4** tbsp sour cream
- **3/4** tsp baking soda
- **1/2** tsp clove
- **1/2** tsp ginger
- **1/2** tsp salt
- **2** c flour
- **2** c oatmeal

1. Mix all ingredient in large mixing bowl until mixed well.

2. Spoon mixture on to greased cookie sheet.

3. Bake at 375° F for 8 minutes.

SNICKERDOODLE

Serving Size: 12

- **1 1/2** c sugar
- **1** c butter
- **2** eggs
- **2 3/4** c flour
- **2** tsp cream of tartar
- **1** tsp of baking soda
- **1/4** tsp salt

1. Mix all ingredients in a large bowl.

2. Roll into 1.5" balls

3. Roll in a mixture of cinnamon and sugar and place on greased cookie sheet and bake at 375° F for 8 minutes.

CHOCOLATE CHIP COOKIES

Serving Size: 12

6 c flour
1 1/2 sugar
2 brown sugar
4 sticks of butter, melted
3 eggs
1 tsp salt
1/2 tsp baking soda
2 tsp vanilla
1 package chocolate chips

1. Combine sugar, brown sugar, melted butter in large mixing bowl.

2. Beat for 5 minutes.

3. Combine remaining ingredients and mix thoroughly.

4. Bake at 375° F for 8 minutes

PEANUT BUTTER COOKIES

Serving Size: 12

1 c butter
1 c peanut butter
1 c sugar
1 c brown sugar
2 eggs
1 tsp vanilla
3 flour
1 tsp baking soda
1/2 tsp salt

1. Mix ingredients together in large bowl.

2. Roll in 1.5" ball.

3. Roll in additional sugar before baking.

4. Press with fork twice diagonally making criss-cross.

5. Bake at 375° F for 8 minutes

CRÈME BRÛLÉE

Serving Size: 6

Hard exterior and soft on the inside. Kinda like how I like my men. All this dessert needs now is dick. Bon appétit!

- **2** c heavy cream
- **1** ea vanilla bean, scraped
- **1** c sugar
- **6** ea egg yolks
  sugar for torching

1. Preheat oven to 325°F.

2. Set 6 (8oz) ramekins in a roasting pan. Set aside.

3. Bring cream, vanilla to a heavy simmer over medium-high heat.

4. In a bowl, whisk together sugar and egg yolks until pale and doubled in size. Slowly whisk in cream into egg mixture.

5. Divide custard into ramekins. Pour enough hot water into roasting pan to come halfway up the sides of the ramekins.

6. Bake until set but center trembles slightly, approximately 35 to 40 minutes.

7. Transfer to fridge and chill overnight.

8. Before serving, sprinkle an even layer of sugar over the surface of the crème brûlées. Torch the sugar to create a nice amber colored crust. Cool slightly before serving as the ramekins will be hot from the blowtorch.

PRALINE THUMBPRINT COOKIES

Serving Size: 18 - 20

You've done weirder things with your thumb.

---

2 c powdered sugar
2 c butter
4 c flour
1 tbsp vanilla
2 c pecans

SAUCE

1/2 butter
1 cup brown sugar
1/2 cup evaporated milk
1/4 tsp salt
2 cups powdered sugar
1/2 tsp vanilla

---

1. Add ingredients into a small pot and mix together at medium heat.

2. Bring to a boil for 1 minute stirring regularly.

1. Add soften butter into a mixing bowl.

2. Add additional ingredients and stir in slowly.

3. Form 1 · inch balls and place on greased cookie sheet.

4. Use your thumb to make a small imprint in each cookie.

5. Wet your thumb slightly with a dab of water to avoid sticking

6. Bake at 275° for 11 minutes.

7. Spoon small amount of sauce into thumbprints and top with a pecan.

8. Let cool and harden.

OTTERSCOTCH PIE

Serving Size: 8

Fine. It's a Butterscotch Pie. But just as delicious, I promise. No baking required and best served cold, just like my heart.

---

3   whole milk
4   egg yolks beaten
2   brown sugar
2   tsp vanilla
8   tbsp all purpose flour
2   tbsp butter

1. Mix brown sugar and flour in a bowl thoroughly with a fork.

2. Heat milk in heavy pan medium heat

3. Add brown sugar flour mixture into heated milk.

4. Keep stirred regularly as not to stick.

5. When mixture begins to boil take 2 tbsp of mixture and mix with beaten egg yolks.

6. Egg yolks will cook in mixture.

7. Pour mix of eggs back into pan continue heat until mixture is thick and boils for 1 min.

8. Add vanilla and butter.

9. Pour pudding mixture into a baked pie crust.

10. Now Cool.

Use egg whites to make fresh meringue or top with whipped cream.

CITRUS POLENTA

Serving Size: 8 - 10

1 c medium grain polenta
2 c almond meal
1 1/2 tsp baking powder
1/2 tsp salt
1 stick unsalted, sweet cream butter, softened
1 c sugar
3 ea eggs
1 tsp vanilla extract
1/2 c natural yogurt
2 ea lemons, zested (save juice for syrup)

LEMON HONEY SYRUP

1/2 c honey
juice from 2 lemons
3 ea sprigs of thyme
orange mascarpone:
1 (8 to 9 oz) container of mascarpone cheese
1 ea lg orange, zested
2 tbsp powdered sugar
1 tbsp fresh squeezed orange juice

1. Mix all together.

2. Roll into 1.5 inch balls.

3. Roll balls in a mixture of cinnamon and sugar

4. Place on greased cookie sheet and bake at 375°F for 8 minutes

---

1. In a mixer, cream together butter and sugar until light and fluffy.

2. Add eggs 1 at a time. Mix in vanilla. Fold in yogurt and zest.

3. Add dry ingredients into wet until incorporated. Do not over mix.

4. Pour batter into pan and smooth the top with a rubber spatula. Bake for 30 minutes, then turn the oven down to 325°F and bake for another 15 to 20 minutes, or until toothpick inserted comes out almost clean with a few crumbs sticking to it.

5. Cool completely and prick all over with a toothpick.

6. For the syrup, combine all ingredients into a small sauce pan and bring to a boil. Remove thyme and brush hot syrup over cooled cake.

7. For the orange mascarpone topping, whip all together and serve a small dollop or quenelle atop each slice of cake.

NEW YORK STYLE CHEESECAKE

Serving Size: 6

CRUST

1 1/2	c graham cracker crumbs
3	tbsp sugar
1/2	tbsp cinnamon
1/4	c butter

1. Combine ingredients and press into bottom of springform pan.

2. Bake at 400°F for 4 minutes

FILLING

4	packages cream cheese
2	tbsp flour
1/4	tsp salt
1 1/4	c sugar
1/2	c sour cream
1	tbsp vanilla essence
3	large eggs

1. Combine cream cheese, flour, and salt in a large mixing bowl.

2. Beat until smooth.

3. Add sugar, sour cream, and vanilla.

4. Beat until well blended.

5. Add eggs, one at a time.

6. Pour mixture into crust.

7. Bake until slightly firm but still has a jiggle when pan is shaken

A P P L E   P I E

Serving Size: 6 - 8

All American, just like baseball or silicone implants. Few things will ever beat the classics. Enjoy this warm, moist delicacy with a scoop of vanilla ice cream and join me in living the American Dream. Getting ass implants.

---

1 ea prepared 9" crust, par cooked + extra dough for lattice top

8 ea granny smith apples, peeled, cored, and sliced 1/4" thick

1/2 c packed brown sugar

2 tbsp AP flour

2 tsp grated cinnamon stick

1 pinch of nutmeg

1 vanilla bean, scraped

1 tbsp lemon juice

2 tbsp unsalted butter

1. Preheat oven to 400°F.

2. Combine all ingredients, except pie crust and butter into a bowl and toss.

3. Pour filling into prepared pie crust. Dot with butter and cover with lattice.

4. Brush top with butter and sprinkle with sugar.

5. Bake for 35 to 40 minutes until bubbly.

RASPBERRY JELLO SALAD

Serving Size: 15

Fruits, nuts, and cream. Sounds like a fun weekend. Or a Raspberry Jello Salad. Either way, here is a salad I know you'll love. And like that hot guy on the pole, you may not get to toss it, but you can appreciate the jiggle.

---

1 large pkg, raspberry gelatin
2 boiling water
1 package frozen raspberries
2 large bananas mashed
1 can crushed pineapple
1 c chopped pecans
1 pint sour cream

1. Dissolve gelatin in boiling water. Add raspberries followed the mashed bananas and can of crushed pineapple with juice.

2. Mix well.

3. Add pecans and mix again.

4. Pour half of the mixture into a 9x13 glass baking dish.

5. Refrigerate until firm.

6. Once firm remove from the refrigerator and spread 1/4" of sour cream over firm jello evenly.

7. Pour the remaining mixture over the top. Refrigerate until firm and you are good to go mister man!

PANNA COTTA WITH HONEY GELEE

Serving Size: 8

I have a confession. I might be a bit of a bear chaser. And nothing attracts bears better than honey, right? So I'm preparing my famous Panna Cotta with Honey Glaze. I can stand to be mauled for the evening. Till then I'll wait patiently. I'm just a regular bear trap.

1 1/4 c heavy cream
1 1/4 c milk
1/4 c sugar
1/4 c honey
1 ea vanilla bean, scraped
3 ea sheets of gelatin

FOR THE FILLING

1 ea gelatin sheet
1/3 c honey
1 c water

1. In a saucepan, combine cream, milk, vanilla, honey, and sugar. Bring to a simmer.

2. In a bowl of cool water, place sheets of gelatin in to soften. Set aside.

3. When the cream mix begins to steam, pull gelatin and squeeze out excess water. Stir gelatin in cream and stir until dissolved.

4. Remove from heat and into a cool water bath, no ice.

5. Divide into 4oz , leaving a 1" gap from the rim for the gelee. Chill for 3 to 4 hours. After the panna cotta has chilled, start the gelee.

6. Soak 1 sheet of gelatin in a bowl of cool water. Set aside.

7. In a saucepan, bring water and honey to a boil, stirring constantly. Remove from heat, and add gelatin.

8. Place pot in a cool water bath.

9. Pour gelee over panna cotta and chill for 2 hours. Serve cold.

SUGAR FREE STRAWBERRY CUPCAKES

Serving Size: 24

Who doesn't enjoy a good drag show? Can these bitches look any more like the real thing? Today, Farrah Moan is teaching you how to make Sugar Free Cupcakes. You'll love them. And like Farrah, I bet you won't be able to tell the difference. Careful straight boys.

2 3/4	c cake flour
1/4	tsp salt
2 1/2	tsp baking powder
1	(3oz) pkg sugar free strawberry gelatin
2	sticks of unsalted butter, softened
1 1/4	c honey
4	ea eggs, room temperature
1/4	c strawberry puree
1/2	c milk, room temperature
1	ea vanilla bean, scraped
1/3	c freeze-dried strawberries, crushed

1. Sift together flour, salt, and baking powder. In a mixer, cream together butter and gelatin until light and fluffy. Add eggs one at a time.

2. Combine milk, vanilla and puree. Add flour mixture alternately with milk mixture to mixer in batches, starting and ending with flour mixture. Fold in strawberries.

3. Bake in lined cupcake pan for 18 to 20 minutes or until toothpick inserted comes out clean. Let cool.

4. Frost with your favorite sugar free frosting, and garnish with fresh strawberries.

Some sugar is naturally occuring in strawberry puree and honey

I started off as such a classy bitch last night.
What happened? Chances are, someone was taking
pictures so I'll probably need to spend the better part
of the morning untagging myself.
That's what friends are for.

But before you go cramming vodka-cranberry or gin
and tonic down your throat again, consider making a
handcrafted cocktail for you and your guests. It could
very well help you slow it down and appreciate the
evening a little more.

Remember, always play safely and sanely while under
the influence of such exotic aphrodisiacs. Alcohol
should enhance the atmosphere, not kidnap it.

What Had Happened Was...

SEX IN THE CITY

Serving Size: Per Drink

When you can't find a beach, try Sex in the City. All the fun without sand in your crack. But don't worry, we'll also teach you how to make Sex on the Beach. Although something tells me you already know how.

1.5 oz of Deep Eddy Cranberry
1.5 oz of Deep Eddy Lemon
.5 oz Chambord
   sour & orange juice
   fresh squeezed lime juice
1 3/4 oz Bacardi Dragonberry
3/4 oz 151 Rum

1. Cranberry juice and sweet & sour equal parts.

2. Pour in shaker, chill it, pour on rocks and end with a splash of sprite on top.

3. Garnish with lime wedge or strawberry.

DAIQUIRI

Serving Size: Per Drink

---

2 oz Bacardi White Rum
1 oz simple syrup
1 oz lime juice

1. Combine all ingredients in shaker and twerk til chilled.

2. Strain into a martini glass, garnish with lime wedge, and enjoy!

WATERMELON AMORTINI

You know what tequila does to me. Bring it on.

---

2 oz Amorada Blanco Tequila
1 oz Grand Marnier
1 oz fresh orange juice
1 oz fresh watermelon puree
(simply blend chunks of watermelon in a blender and do not filter)
1/2 medium lime juice
dash of olive juice

1. Mix all the ingredients in a shaker with ice and shake for about 5 seconds and pour into a martini glass.

2. We ask that you do not serve the Amortini over ice as it will just water it down and change the taste profile.

3. Trust me, it's already strong enough.

PIÑA COLADA

Serving Size: Per Drink

---

2 oz Bacardi White Rum
3 oz pineapple juice
1 oz cream of coconut
1 maraschino cherry
1 pineapple slice

1. Combine rum, pineapple juice, and cream of coconut into blender with ice.

2. Blend for 20 seconds and pour into Poco Grande glass.

3. Garnish with maraschino cherry and pineapple slice.

DIRTY MARTINI

Serving Size: Per Drink

Perfect for the dirty bitch trying to look classy. We're all fooled.

---

2 oz gin
1 tbsp dry vermouth
3 tbsp olive juice
2 olives

1. Add gin, dry vermouth, and olive juice in shaker with two ice cubes.

2. Strain contents into martini glass with two olives

HIGHBALL

Serving Size: Per Drink

---

2 oz whiskey
ginger ale

1. Pour contents on ice.

WICKED COCKTAIL

Bitch, you've always been the wicked witch, don't lie. Now enjoy enough of these wicked cocktails without turning green. Remember my pretty, everything in moderation.

---

1 3/4 oz Bacardi Dragonberry
3/4 oz 151 Rum
cranberry juice and sweet & sour equal parts

1. Pour in shaker, chill it, pour on rocks and end with a splash of sprite on top.

2. Garnish with lemon wedge or strawberry.

SEX ON THE BEACH

1.5 oz vodka
1 oz peach schnapps
1.5 oz orange juice (pineapple works too)
1.5 oz cranberry juice

1. Pour ingredients over ice in a highball glass.

2. Mix well and garnish with an orange wheel.

STRAWBERRY MINT JULEP

Serving Size: Per Drink

Drink your juice, Shelby.

2 large ripe strawberries, washed and hulled
2 teaspoons sugar (or more to taste)
2 oz Amorada Reposado Tequila
mint leaves

1. Muddle 1 strawberry and 2 mint leaves in a julep tumbler or similar glass, about 10 to 12 ounces in size.

2. Add 1 teaspoon sugar and a small amount of Amorada Reposado (about 2 to 3 teaspoons); stir until sugar is dissolved. Fill glass or tumbler half full with crushed ice.

3. Add remaining Amorada Reposado; until blended. Fill glass with crushed ice. Stir, not touching with hands, until the cup frosts.

4. Cut remaining strawberry in slices; use to garnish the julep. Garnish with a sprig of mint.

MOSCOW MULE

Serving Size: Per Drink

1.5 oz vodka
1 bottle ginger beer

1. Mix into crushed ice.

2. Serve in copper mug and garnish with lemon wedge.

HURRICAINE

Serving Size: Per Drink

It took your house, car, and all your designer socks. Not an actual hurricane, but your ex. If you're in need of relief, don't look to FEMA. Have an ice cold, refreshing, fruit inspired hurricane to ease the pain. You'll be ready for the next storm.

1 oz dark rum
1 oz white rum
2 oz passion fruit syrup
2 tbsp simple syrup
1 oz orange juice
1 oz lime juice
1 maraschino cherry

1. Shake in mixer with cubed ice.

2. Pour into hurricane glass with crushed ice.

3. Garnish with orange wheel and top with maraschino cherry.

.

MUDSLIDE

Serving Size: Per Drink

1 oz Tito's Vodka
1 oz Bailey's Irish cream
1 oz Kahlua Coffee Liqueur
1 oz cream

1. Combine all ingredients into shaker with cubed or crushed ice.

2. Shake and pour all contents into tall glass.

STRAWBERRY MOJITO

Serving Size: Per Drink

Hey Rummy! Beat the heat with this refreshing twist by adding strawberry purée to this already delicious mojito mix.

2 oz white rum	1. Add strawberries, mint and sugar into mixer, muddle thoroughly.
7-10 mint leave	
1 teaspoon of sugar	2. Add rum crushed ice and top with club soda.
1 oz fresh lime juice	
	3. Stir or shake.
	4. Pour entire contents into glass.
	5. Garnish with strawberry and mint leaves.

BLOODY MARY

Serving Size: Per Drink

2 oz. Tito's Vodka	1. Pour liquid ingredients into glass and stir.
4 oz. tomato juice	
2 dashes Tabasco Sauce	2. Add desired amount of pepper.
1/2 teaspoon of Worcestershire sauce	
ground black pepper to taste	3. Pour into salted rim glass.
1 slice thick cut bacon cooked	
1 stalk celery	4. Add olives, celery, and bacon slice.
3 olives	

A P P L E T I N I

Serving Size: Per Drink

We all remember the forbidden fruit. It was pulled straight from the Tree of Knowledge. And after all them appletinis, we still haven't made the best decisions. Either way, I say we toast! *"Here's to the men who make stiff drinks and here's to the drinks that make men stiff... cheers!"*

2 oz Absolut Vodka
1 oz apple brandy
apple juice

1. Mix vodka and apple brandy and apple juice in shaker with crushed ice.

2. Pour into martini glass using strainer.

3. Garnish with thinly sliced green apples.

4. Get turnt bitch!

C H A M P A G N E
C O C K T A I L

Serving Size: Per Drink

1/2 oz cognac
1/2 oz Grand Marnier

1. Top with your favorite brut champagne.

OLD FASHIONED

Serving Size: Per Drink

Don't fist on the first date? You must be old fashioned. (No, but seriously, thank you for hanging in there this far). If you're in the mood for a sophisticated beverage with the perfect amount of kick, look no further.

---

2 teaspoons simple syrup
1 teaspoon water
2 dashes bitters
1 c ice cubes
1.5 oz jigger bourbon whiskey
1 slice orange
2 maraschino cherry

1. Pour the simple syrup, water, and bitters into a whiskey glass.

2. Stir to combine, then place the ice cubes in the glass.

3. Pour bourbon over the ice and garnish with the orange slice and maraschino cherry.

TOM COLLINS

Serving Size: Per Drink

---

2 oz gin
1 oz lemon juice
2 maraschino cherry
club soda
simple syrup
orange wheel

1. Pour g in and lemon juice over ice.

2. Mix in simple syrup to taste.

3. Fill remainder of glass with club soda.

4. Garnish with lemon and a maraschino cherry.

Work Hard, Play Hard. Well, I guess they should have mentioned "Repeat". Time to get back on track before the desserts and cocktails catch up and get the best of your boyish figure.

These delicious protein shakes, fruit smoothies and veggie juices will help you bounce back, ready to take on anything, no matter how big.

Recovery

BERRY NICE SMOOTHIE

Serving Size: Per Drink

2 c frozen or fresh mixed berries
1 c plain yogurt
2 c crushed ice

1. Add all contents to blender.

2. Blend and enjoy, queen.

COCO DELIGHT

Serving Size: Per Drink

1 banana
1 oz coconut shavings
2 tbsp coconut oil
2 oz coconut cream
1/2 c coconut milk
1 c ice

1. Add all contents to blender.

2. Blend and enjoy, queen.

HUNKY MONKEY

Serving Size: Per Drink

Make the most of your post workout with this yummy protein packed smoothie.

---

1 banana
2 tbsp crunchy peanut butter
1 c ice
1 c water
1 c milk
2 scoops chocolate whey protein

1. Blend all ingredients for 30 seconds.

2. Enjoy

PEACH MANGO

Serving Size: Per Drink

---

1 c frozen peaches
1 banana
1 c chopped mango
1 c plain yogurt

1. Blend all ingredients for 30 seconds.

2. Add stevia to increase sweetness.

GREEN MEAN MACHINE

Serving Size: Per Drink

---

3 stalks celery
1 granny smith apple
1 cucumber
2 tbsp peeled and chopped ginger
1 c chopped kale
1 lemon
1 c chopped collard greens
1 oz chopped parsley

1. Add all ingredients into vegetable juicer.

2. Serve cold drink immediately.

ALMOND MELON CRUSH

Serving Size: Per Drink

---

2 c honeydew melon
1 c almond milk
1 c ice
2 tbsp honey

1. Blend ingredients and enjoy.

FLOWER COUTURE

CORDELIA DE CASTELLANE

FLOWER COUTURE

FROM MY GARDEN TO MY HOUSE

New York · Paris · London · Milan

Le Jardin
de
Cordelia

CONTENTS

MY COUNTRY HOUSE

MY COLORS

My daily uniform seems to be limited to navy, black, gray, white, or beige. I can't give you too much fashion advice as my tastes are pretty conservative and boring. Color catches the eye, so I prefer it in my collections, my creations, and even in my garden.

Bunny Mellon, the famous American horticulturist said, "Flowers were my life; they spoke for me when I couldn't." It's flowers that speak to me best about color, nuance, and harmony.

I don't mix more than three colors together at one time because it would be too risky to control. That's how I came up with the idea of describing flowers through their shades. It was a real puzzle. To be honest, I don't see colors in the same way as other people. Could this be a form of color blindness? (I really shouldn't write that.)

Then came the classification of ochres, saffrons, and gingerbreads. And white? What kind of white are we talking about? It's not white, it's cream, snow, pearl, grainy, gray, and so many more. It's precisely these infinite nuances that fascinate me. In my studio, jars of candies remind me of flowers and guide the colors in my collections.

My next step will be to make my own plant-based dyes. An infinite palette is terribly tempting. Sometimes life is far too hard to be seen only in black and white.

THE DREAM WORLD OF MY GARDEN

There are undoubtedly many more feelings in this garden
than there are flowers.

In a very personal way, the particular period of Covid brought me face
to face with mourning my father, who had died a few months before.
It's here in this garden that I've poured out my grief. It seems that working
the earth can be the best psychologist in the world. I believe this is true.

Flowers have always been my best friends; I can't imagine a home without
flowers. The idea of having a garden full of these pretty ladies appealed
to me a lot, with their inimitable color palettes, their grace,
and their fragility. All this at my fingertips.

I spent a lot of time in the middle of mountain meadows when I was
growing up. My grandmother and I used to make herbariums with flowers
pressed inside huge dictionaries—when those books weren't balanced
on my head for perfect posture, as she liked to do, or to measure myself
or look up each word that I discovered in books. Perhaps, in the end,
words and flowers grew together with me.

The world of gardening has plunged me into a new life. I'm a woman
in a hurry—impatient and controlling—so I'm learning to become patient
and to observe what nature decides for me.

I am afraid of insects and spiders, and earthworms disgust me! But suddenly
I put my hands in the earth and delight in finding myself covered in mud.

I quit the Instagram fashion show accounts without a care, and now
I follow all the landscapers and gardeners for advice. I'm discovering
a garden community that I love far more than any magazine cover or fancy
dinner. This is how I discovered Milan Hajsinek, who would go on to design
the garden of my dreams with the finesse that I am known for. I recognize
that I don't know much about it, but I'm learning and persevering every day.

At last I've joined Christian Dior in his passion, and the prints inherited
from Emanuel Ungaro have become even more meaningful to me. Nature
takes pride of place in my creativity. My life is more relaxed, which allows
me to focus on what I love most after my family and my imagination.

This garden has transformed my life.
There's nothing extraordinary about it;
it is small and pretty, but it's given me a passion.
I'll take you there. There are so many secrets
and there is so much love behind my little wooden gate.

BOUQUETS MY WAY

As with everything in my life, I make my bouquets by feeling. I am not a florist
—far from it—which is why I like to work with the best people, like the famous Parisian
florist Éric Chauvin or my talented English friend, Willow Crossley.

I make my bouquets in the country on Friday evenings or early Saturday mornings.
It's probably my favorite appointment of the week. I put on some music, gather the flowers
together like small groups of friends having fun, and dive into my own world.

There are big flowers, small flowers, pretentious flowers, arrogant flowers, fragile flowers,
ugly flowers, and very beautiful flowers.

You have to appreciate and balance it all—like everything in life. Mind you, when I say
"balance," I'm not fond of bouquets composed at the same height like a sphere. I don't like
anything too slick. I only know how to make bouquets in vases or baskets, not without
a container like florists do.

Here are some little sketches showing my weekend bouquet-making routine. The bouquets
often turn up in my little Coffee Flower Shop or in the prints I design for Dior. I photograph
them and zoom in on them. I steal everything from them—from their shapes to their colors
to their hearts. They're too beautiful to let go.

FIG. 1
Sheaf

I really like to keep the shape of the flowers
simple. I always enjoy the asymmetry of a bouquet
falling over the edge of a mantelpiece. They're also
pretty on the corners of high furniture.

FIG. 2
Rustic

Naturally, this is what I do most often.
High, tall, and free, with bold combinations
from the morning's pickings. I play with heights
and colors, and I imagine great conversations.

FIG. 3
Wreath

Inspired by the Middle Ages, when wreaths
adorned large village festivals and celebrations.
I love wreaths for Christmas and made with
mimosa or spring flowers too. I often tie a bow
on them and hang them on doors in the country;
they can be made with dried flowers
and used all season long.

FIG. 4
Couture

I hate round bouquets, which are too perfect for
my flowers. These ladies are too temperamental,
so I call my more structured bouquets "couture,"
usually arranged with roses from the garden.
I like them small, in tumblers and small vases.
I also love this shape for peonies.

FIG. 5
Wild

I sometimes come across incredible branches,
tall grasses, and unexpected wild flowers on
my walks. If it won't damage the natural order,
I use my pruning shears, gather my finds under
my arm, and place them in a large, heavy vase that
supports their weight. These huge wild bouquets
often take up all the light in the room.

FIG. 6
Flowing

The *atelier flou* is where flowing haute couture
dresses are made. Don't imagine an untidy
bouquet when you read that word. A flowing
bouquet is poetic. Extremely precious flowers
are chosen and positioned carefully in a vase,
with contrasts in the height and spacing
so that each one can shine.

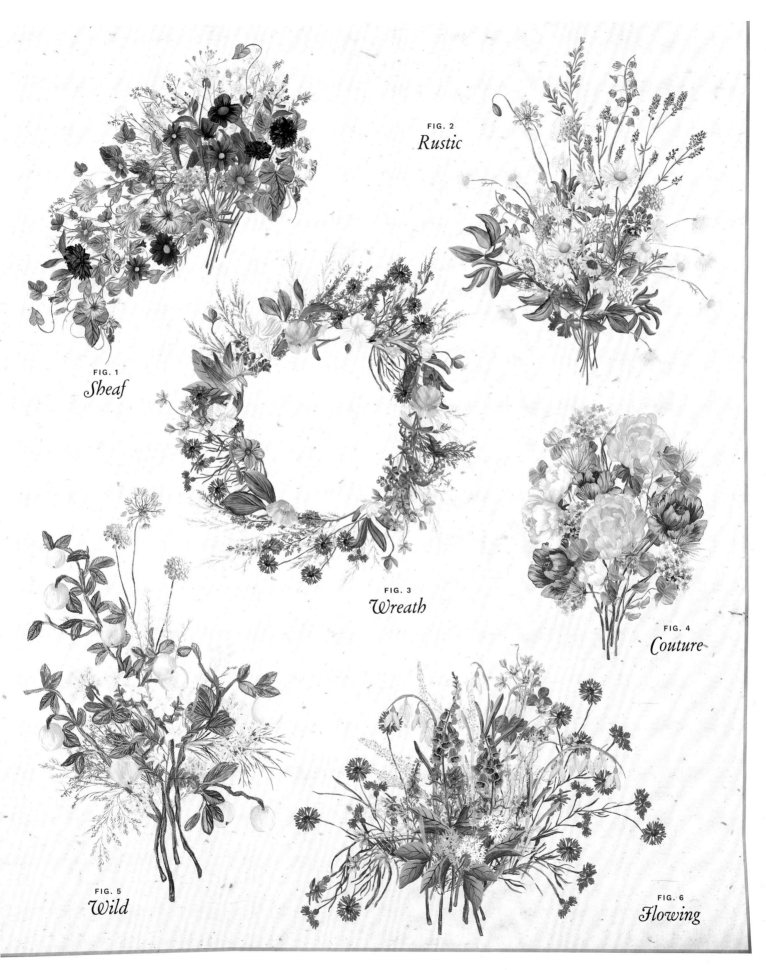

FIG. 2
Rustic

FIG. 1
Sheaf

FIG. 3
Wreath

FIG. 4
Couture

FIG. 5
Wild

FIG. 6
Flowing

ELEVATING
MY FLOWERS

There are no rules for showcasing these beauties.

I like to use all kinds of vases and containers. Of course,
I have a passion for wicker cachepots, old antique flea market
baskets, glass or ceramic carafes, my grandmother's large soup
tureens, gravy boats, and Clichy vases I've collected.

Anything but the obvious, though a big, beautiful vase is always
fun for my maxi-bouquets when I go crazy! I have a penchant
for blown glass or crystal bud vases set on tables. I see them
like beautiful knights that make the flower ladies dance.

Since I was very young, I've been collecting little hyacinth vases
that I just love. Dior makes them in all sorts of colors. They work
for round, soft bouquets in the bathroom or on bedside tables,
especially with garden roses or peonies.

The porcelain teacup too ... I make little arrangements
with flowers I happen to find on the ground. I think I'm totally
old-fashioned. I like flowers that are out of fashion, forgotten.
For a long time, I was the only person with a passion for dahlias
and irises in faded, almost aged colors, and sunflowers that
remind me of the pretty farmhouses I knew during
my childhood in Switzerland.

I'll transform anything as long as it can hold water, and if it's not
watertight, I place a glass inside, even one the size of a shot glass.

Cups become vases for lilies of the valley set on tea trays
or in baskets; bunches of snapdragons in shades of pink.
Sometimes it all falls apart ...

I prefer not to count certain things in my life, like my vases,
my plates, or my glasses. Champagne glasses make lovely
containers for wildflowers, for example. When I have trouble
making them stand up, I use my flower frogs (the secret
behind everything) or chicken wire to make
my large bouquets appear fuller.

Corolla

Small Bottles

Russian

Stemmed Glass

Faceted

Flute

Bubble Carafe

Pumpkin Pitcher

Periwinkle

Galileo

Cleopatra

Butterflies

Diamond

Bell-shaped
Bud Vases

Flora

Bamboo

Tokyo

Amaryllis

Valencia

Directoire

Gourd

Dragon

Acacia

Floréal

Dragonfly

Orchid

Wisteria

Iris

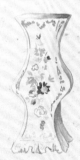

Narcissus

Jasmine

Hyacinth

Physalis

Victoria

Empire

Amphora

Garden Basket

Wicker

Reed

Easter

Watering Can

Soup Tureen

Porcelain Teacup

Braided Jug

Gravy Boat

Farmhouse Jug

MY COFFEE FLOWER SHOP

It really wasn't meant to be! A folly, madness, a whim …

I could tell you a lovely tale about wanting to bring part of my country house to Paris.
I'd been looking for the perfect place and thinking about my concept in detail.
It would make a poetic story. But here's how this sweet little burden
really came to life …

A friend said to me, "If I hadn't done this job, I would have been a florist." I replied
"That's funny, me too. It's a dream that I've kept buried." But it's true that as I said it,
I felt it deeply. "Since you're already a florist, you and your garden, you just need
a shop," he replied, laughing. "But, above all, serve us a cup of tea while we wait for
our bouquet. There are always hours of waiting around at the florist." And then
a guardian angel whispered to me: "You know that in Los Angeles, there are coffee
shops that sell flowers?" Photos came flooding in on my phone. "Oh, you know me
and retail … I don't know how to manage anything. I just want to create." A day later,
he found a pop-up shop on rue du Bac: "It's on the corner of your street.
You can try it for three months."

So, I launched my Christmas wreaths at the café, and they were shipped
all over Europe. During the Christmas holidays, I used the money to finance
a few renovations, and in January we launched the Coffee Flower Shop.

I train wonderful florists. Or rather, I untrain them, passing on my totally
nontechnical way of imagining and creating bouquets, always with the conviction
that, like my decorations, everything should be the same as it is at home.
For me, a natural and effortless aesthetic is key to any successful decoration,
and the same goes for the way I like to arrange flowers.

The coffee side of things is taken care of by friends with a bit more experience
than me, who bring in Italian machines, coffee, baristas, and lots of things I didn't
even know existed until now. My son Stanislas, a chef, came to my rescue and
perfected the cake recipes to add to the homemade spirit. As for my son Andreas,
who's much more financially minded, he looked at my concept and wondered
how it was going to stand up financially.

But the challenge was on, and I only had a few months to show that we could pull
this off with our heads held high, and find out if we could turn this pop-up into
a longer-term boutique. We're still writing the story today, slowly and surely,
and thanks to the enormous support of all my customers, I think we can say
that we've just about pulled it off.

I'm very pleased to have been able to create a peaceful place that provides a real
break from the stress of Parisian life, where people like to come, relax, and eat cake,
surrounded by the beauty of the best ladies-in-waiting on earth, those wonderful
flowers that are with us in every season.

They are delivered three times a week directly from my country house,
forty-five minutes from Paris, picked that very morning. We don't use any chemicals
in the garden, in the soil, or on the flowers. Everything is completely natural.

I really enjoy getting a taste of what the fascinating, though extremely hard and
testing, agricultural life is like. Our countries need farmers, and we need to save
our soil before it's too late. It puts things very much in perspective for me, far from
my everyday world, and trying to participate in these essential changes has become
a big part of my life. This boutique is also part of that message!

MY GARDEN FAIRIES

People often ask me how I manage to do so much. I'm lucky enough to work with incredible teams who are often stronger than me in certain areas.

I know exactly what I want and have very clear and definite ideas in my work. It's very different in my life, where I want everything and its opposite. But there's one thing that always comes back around, which is, it has to be "fast."

My home "garden team," which is slowly growing, had a good laugh about that. In the garden, we can't decide anything. We have to wait, often for years. It's a great learning experience for me: becoming more patient. We discover a lot together, because for some of us, being gardeners was a change of direction. But that's what I like—the teamwork where we try to innovate and understand together. We plant and sometimes we fail; we follow tips on Instagram or ask our gardening friends for advice. We're making great progress.

It's true that my garden is like a baby to me, and when the weather gets rough, I can get very emotional.

One day, in the middle of April, Laurent (who looks after the house and garden) warned me that snow was coming. I left all my meetings. In an hour, we protected all the tulips with car covers and garbage bags … with anything we could find. We still smile about it, but we saved those beautiful ladies.

I'd like to thank the adorable country team for putting so much heart into their work. The garden feels it and the results are pretty good!

CHAPTER 1

THE GRASS OF MY CHILDHOOD

Green

THE GRASS OF MY CHILDHOOD

Green awakens and a silent promise unfolds. The first timid shoots appear after the rain, a leaf opens up in the sun. A murmur of hope runs through the fields as far as the eye can see: a symphony of shades, from the tender green of young shoots to the deep green of ancient forests.

Green is life pulsating, the vibrant energy of nature constantly renewing itself. It's the fresh smell of damp moss, the rustle of the wind in the trees, the melodious song of birds hidden in the foliage. Green soothes the soul and replenishes the body and mind. It is a refuge of peace and serenity, and an invitation to contemplation and harmony with the world around us.

I hated green for a long time, probably out of superstition, and then one day I discovered it and fell in love.

Buxus sempervirens

— BOXWOOD —

With its evergreen foliage, boxwood has been considered a symbol of eternity since Gallo-Roman times. The art of topiary originated from a desire to master nature by giving it ornamental form. A famous anecdote mentions Gaius Matius, friend of the emperor Augustus, who was among the first to prune shrubs into geometric shapes in Roman gardens. This art evolved over time, reaching its apogee during the Renaissance. At Versailles, under Louis XIV, André Le Nôtre used topiaries to structure the gardens, drawing attention to the perfect alliance between nature and architecture. These plant sculptures became a symbol of prestige and harmony.

TYPE *Shrub*

SOIL *Rich to limestone*

FLOWERING *April to May*

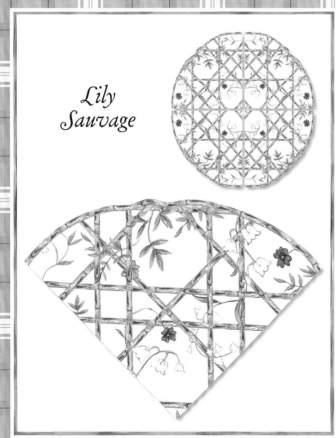

Lily Sauvage

At home, I do things instinctively,
arranging tables at the last minute without
thinking about it too much.
At Dior, I like to take the time to design
the décor and scenography, invent a story,
and immerse myself in the place.

I work on my tables like paintings:
innovating, reinventing myself, surprising
people, and making them happy without
straying too far from good taste. It's a fine
line ...

It often all starts with a sketch.
But the best way to see if a décor is
successful is from a photo. This is how
I know my tables work.

SUMMER BOUDOIR

Snapdragons, daisies, Queen Anne's lace

I often use this Dior vase decorated with lily of the valley,
the House's trademark flower. It's ideal for gathering wildflowers.

Green and white tones. Light, wild. I don't fasten any branches
and instead let them fall naturally to the sides. The larger ones
are wedged in the center to give the bouquet height.

The daisies liven things up with their yellow eyes. I arrange them
at the end as if they were jewels, like a final accessory! Above all,
I try to avoid order and symmetry and like to keep small daisies
for the base of the vase.

THE VEGETABLE GARDEN TABLE

Sometimes it's too hot to put a lot of flowers on the table or we may just not have many. I play around with everything— knickknacks, books, and loads of objects that I repurpose.

For lunch that day under the pergola, I brought out my collection of miniature antique baskets and created a décor on a simple tablecloth that looks like a vintage dish towel.

You need an understated tablecloth when you use colors like red, otherwise you can quickly tip over into something a little garish or vulgar.

I prefer to keep it simple with my local produce; they are the stars here. I arrange tomato plants in silver tumblers to contrast with the rustic baskets and tablecloth.

Tomatoes, peppers, and eggplants—there are so many beautiful colors in my centerpiece; also bunches of basil and sometimes even vases of kale.

It looks delectable, and it highlights the harvest and the fresh food on the plate. I match the menu, of course.

I love to use plates with a thousand stories from the garden for both formal dinners and family occasions. It's important to have multifunctional tableware.

Even if the crockery is white, imagine gazpacho served in a bowl or ice-cold lettuce soup—then the touch of color is there!

If you want to avoid red, another idea is a green table with apples, kale, and a few hydrangeas.

It's true that in this book I show you my real everyday tables, though it would probably be more fascinating to show you Dior's sumptuous tables for two hundred people, bedecked with a thousand and one flowers. Those tables are like paintings that require a lot of thought. My idea here is to share ideas that are easy to reproduce, or at least to explain to you my way of doing things. I think you should never make event tables at home.

To support your flowers,
a bell-shaped structure for
peonies or a sweet pea stake
made out of wicker can be
an excellent solution.
There are many tutorials
on Instagram to guide you
in creating these elegant and
practical structures.

MY FAVORITE FLOWERS

FIG. 1
Anemone

Messenger of the winds, the anemone blooms
gracefully in the spring light. Its delicate petals
as fragile as silk capture ephemeral beauty.
A flower of renewal, it reminds us that every
moment, however fleeting, is a wonder
to be savored.

FIG. 2
Cornflower

Humble flower of the fields, the cornflower offers
its azure petals like an echo of the sky. A symbol
of tenderness and memories, it embodies
the simple, discreet beauty of the end of spring.

FIG. 3
Iris

With its majesctic colors, the iris adorns the
cover of my book. Its delicate petals capture
light and catch the eye of the curious passer-by.
Symbolizing wisdom and hope and inviting us to
discover the ideas hidden within each page.

FIG. 4
Hyacinth

Exuding an intoxicating fragrance, the hyacinth,
with its clusters of flowers, from a deep blue to
a delicate pink, rises gracefully, celebrating the
joy of loving and dedication. It illuminates sunny
days, heralding joyous beginnings.

FIG. 5
Daffodil

Golden glow of the first spring flowers, daffodil
rises like a ray of sunlight over an earth still
asleep. Its luminous petals herald the rebirth
of nature, celebrating joy and sharing.
It invites hearts to awaken to the beauty
that is reborn all around.

FIG. 6
Peony

Delicate opulence, the peony blooms in silky balls
of rich, bewitching color. Its intoxicating scent
evokes love and beauty, recalling the sweetness
of memories and the intensity of emotions
in life's precious moments.

FIG. 7
Lily of the Valley

With its fragrant white bell-shaped flowers,
lily of the valley symbolizes gentleness.
It embodies Christian Dior for me, and his iconic
collections, symbolizing luck and happiness.
Its delicate notes whisper promises of renewal
and love, celebrating the beauty of simple
moments with a touch of refinement.

FIG. 8
Tulip

Garden queen, the tulip blooms gracefully
in an array of shimmering colors. With more
than one hundred varieties in my garden, they
recall joy and passion dancing in the breeze. The
flower of love and friendship, the tulip reminds me
that every moment deserves to be celebrated.

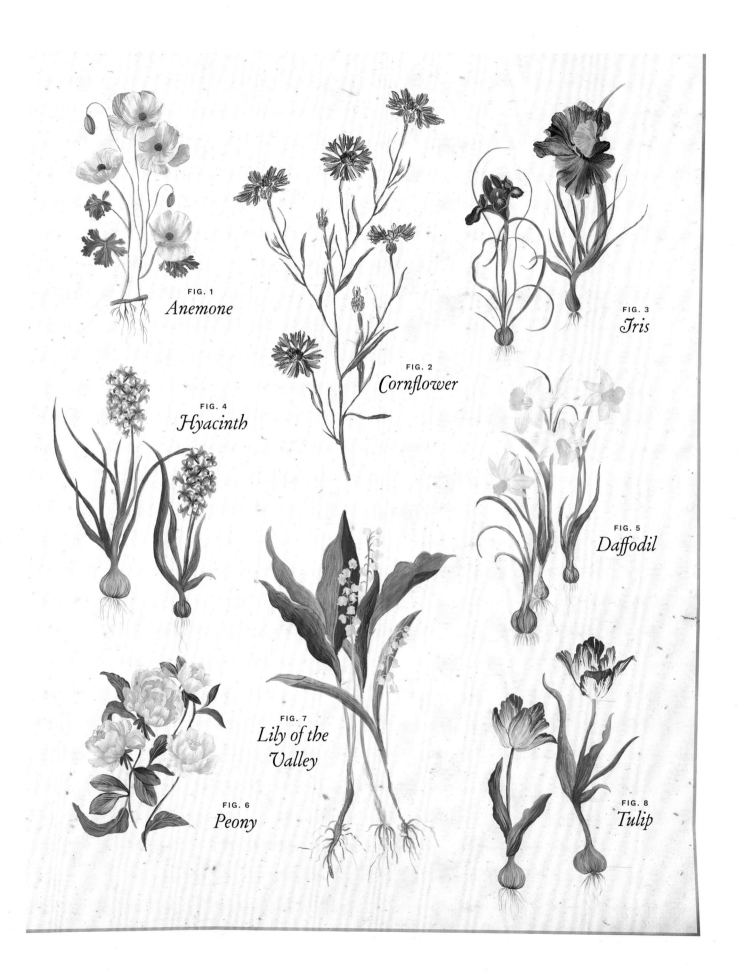

FIG. 1
Anemone

FIG. 2
Cornflower

FIG. 3
Iris

FIG. 4
Hyacinth

FIG. 5
Daffodil

FIG. 7
Lily of the Valley

FIG. 6
Peony

FIG. 8
Tulip

CHAPTER 2

A ROYAL HUE

Purple

A ROYAL HUE

Papa loved wearing purple socks.

I love the grace of violets. Purple is a stirring
color that accentuates everything! It's also
the color of royalty.

I don't decorate anything with purple,
not a room, a piece of clothing, or a sofa,
but I cherish it in my bouquets and in my
garden. I love irises and alliums in the
garden and in vases.

I even put this color on the cover of
this book! Purple is that special touch!
The magic touch in my vases and
on Papa's feet.

When lilacs gently come into season,
my stays here in the countryside grow
longer. I'm always frustrated by their short
existence, yet they transform this place
into a novel-like setting. And thus begins
the dance of purple, lilac,
and lavender blue.

The irises invite themselves along
and dance in groups of different shades,
while mischievous alliums make an
appearance. Snapdragons tower above us.

Some flowers move me, others
fascinate or dazzle me, and others
still make me laugh.

Alliums give gardens and bouquets
a childlike air that seems to announce
good weather. I place them in bud vases,
upright like soldiers, or mix them into
romantic bouquets.

Lavandula angustifolia

— LAVENDER —

Lavender, as we know it today, has its origins in the Mediterranean region. Often prized for its fragrance, it played an important role in ancient Egyptian funeral rites and was famous in ancient Rome for its antiseptic properties. The Romans used it for wellness purposes. Its role moved toward medicine and magic in the Middle Ages. Over time, it became a symbol of peace, purification, and healing. I place lavender sachets in drawers and cupboards throughout the house.

TYPE   *Evergreen sub-shrub*

SOIL   *Neutral*

FLOWERING   *May to August*

Choux
à la violette

I like to incorporate details from
my garden into my baked goods.
These choux à la violette are a
perfect example. They're a splendid
combination of floral elegance
and delightful flavor. Violet is surely
one of my favorite fragrances, rich but
at the same time so sweet. It reminds
me of my childhood in Switzerland.
Syrups and natural violet flavors
are always a nice touch that I like
to add to this recipe. Not forgetting
the ornamental violet flowers,
of course!

MISCHIEVOUS GIRLS

Irises, alliums, wild sweet peas, lavender

Irises are my favorite flowers, so when they come into season,
I get out my barbotine vases decorated with them.

For my arrangements, I like to line up all my vases,
which I choose according to the flowers. Here, I pick tall,
thin, and strong vases, because irises and alliums are tall,
thin, and heavy flowers.

I start with the largest flowers and play with the different
heights. I cut the stems of some irises, as I also like them
to sit flush with the vase tops. I don't overcrowd the composition.
I let the alliums and irises, which are very rigid, take pride
of place. The wild sweet peas add softness, which immediately
creates a poetic, disorderly atmosphere. Finally, I slip in a few
sprigs of lavender.

The house and garden, while comprising my family country home, are also my laboratory for ideas, work, and creativity.

I often shoot Dior Maison settings here, as well as Baby Dior advertising campaigns.

I'm moved by this, because this is where I come up with ideas for the collections, and sometimes they begin and end when they are presented here.

I never really separate my life from my work. They're one and the same. My family lives with it, and I thank them for adapting to my passion.

I often wonder if Christian Dior would have liked my roses and enjoyed spending time here in my garden.

LAVENDER LUNCH

I love creating surprises and placing my tables in unexpected places. Here, in the middle of the lavender beds, I set a table for four with a tablecloth found at a flea market. I let nature create the décor; there's no need for anything more.

I match the shades on the tablecloth with the green ceramic slipware; the chairs that I take from the greenhouse are a nod to my woven wicker plant supports.

A matching pot of lavender from my greenhouse stock and that's it.

I add straw hats to protect my guests from the sun. This attention to detail shows how much we care about our guests.

CHAPTER 3

SUNSET

Yellow

SUNSET

From ochre to lemon, I love yellow. It gives volume to tables and designs and adds a touch of sparkle and elegance.

Saffron often adorns my decorations, even at Christmas to match with fir green or gold. The Romans wore it to weddings, but yellow is associated with being a cheater or a traitor, like Judas's robe.

Yellow is light. It's sunshine and joy!

Autumn is coming and some see the decline of the garden, but I love this time of year. I love the melancholy of certain yellows and the joy of sparkling yellow. Daffodils celebrate the arrival of spring and make me smile from the moment they first appear. There's a tradition in England that whoever discovers the first daffodil will be covered in gold for the rest of the year.

For me, nothing quite beats a room
with printed or woven flower wallpaper
and a coir-mat floor. I like simplicity
that creates a certain peace, and there's
a Proustian madeleine in this association
that reassures me.

At home, on my tables with plain
tablecloths or in the plain bedrooms,
flowers always sit in vases or serve
as a detail. They are never far away.

Iris germanica

— IRIS —

The iris, with its elegant flowers, has a rich history dating back to antiquity. Its name derives from the Greek goddess Iris, messenger to the gods and a symbol of beauty and communication. According to legend, she was so beautiful that she transformed herself into a flower to escape the gods, bringing color and radiance to earthly gardens. The ancient Egyptians also worshipped this flower, associating it with royalty and divinity. Today, the iris is prized for its spectacular beauty, evoking joy and mystery in the garden and recalling the connection between nature and the divine. I love these flowers with their pastel and powdery colors; they touch me with their beauty. I like to display them in tall bud vases and contemplate them like sculptures. In spring, they dance in colorful sequences through my garden.

TYPE *Bulbous or perennial*

SOIL *Neutral, well-drained*

FLOWERING *March to June*

MESSY HAIRSTYLES
Dahlias

I rarely combine orange-yellow dahlias with other flowers.
As a general rule, I'm not always in favor of mixing
certain flowers.

Here, in a collection of Sèvres blue porcelain vases, I arrange
these ladies with their explosive hairstyles flush with the tops
of the vases. Volume and size vary from vase to vase. The only
rule is that you mustn't see any stems! And I leave them
as they are, sitting together for great conversations.

SEPTEMBER TABLE

When the table is beautiful, especially if it's made of thick wood like this one, I prefer not to cover it with a tablecloth. Sometimes I even lay the plates down without any place mats.

I arrange sunflowers in oil bottles that I keep. I don't mix the flowers; I leave the sunflowers alone with one another.

I use myriad shades of green, from soft and faded hues through to deep foliage colors. These tones give depth to the tables.

The wooden cutlery echoes the wooden table and chairs.

I often light a fire in the cavernous fireplace to bring warmth to this large room.

MY FAVORITE FLOWERS

FIG. 1
Agapanthus

With its blue and white spheres, agapanthus rises like stars above the ground. Its ethereal beauty embodies serenity and harmony, conjuring the perfect balance between strength and delicacy. A flower of love and grace, it soothes the soul.

FIG. 2
Foxglove

Striking with its long and beautiful ear and its bell-shaped flowers which reminds us of timbles, the foxglove represents ardor and work. We can often find it in shades of white, pink or purple.

FIG. 3
Poppy

A red glow in the heart of the fields, the poppy unfurls with fragile grace. Its light petals float like breath, summoning freedom and gentle summer days. It symbolizes the ephemeral beauty and quiet strength that persists in the moment, and denotes memory and resilience.

FIG. 4
Dahlia

A flower with many faces, the dahlia blooms in my garden and offers an explosion of shapes and bright colors. Distinguished and refined, it adorns my Coffee Flower Shop, embodying diversity and elegance. A flower of strength and dignity, it reminds us that splendor lies in the richness of nuance.

FIG. 5
Jasmine

With its tiny white stars, jasmine emits an entrancing scent. Suggesting night and love, it embodies purity and passion, bringing mystery and serenity in each fragrant breath.

FIG. 6
Sunflower

A flower that chases the light, the sunflower carries the summer sun within it. Its slender stem rises toward the heavens while its golden petals open in a smile. It evokes warm memories and the beauty of an illuminated world. For me, it also symbolizes Switzerland, my home country, where these flowers abound, gilding the landscape with their golden glow.

FIG. 7
Cosmos

Earthly star, the cosmos dances gracefully. Its light petals open into crowns of infinite color. It whispers secrets of harmony, bowing to the wind. Its presence invites us to contemplate the simple beauty of life and to think about each moment as a tribute to the universe.

FIG. 8
Daisy

The white petals of the daisy surround a golden heart, celebrating the simplicity of life. Dancing in the breeze, offering a smile, it recalls the innocence of summer days, evoking the beauty of fleeting moments and the tenderness of childhood memories with its discreet charm.

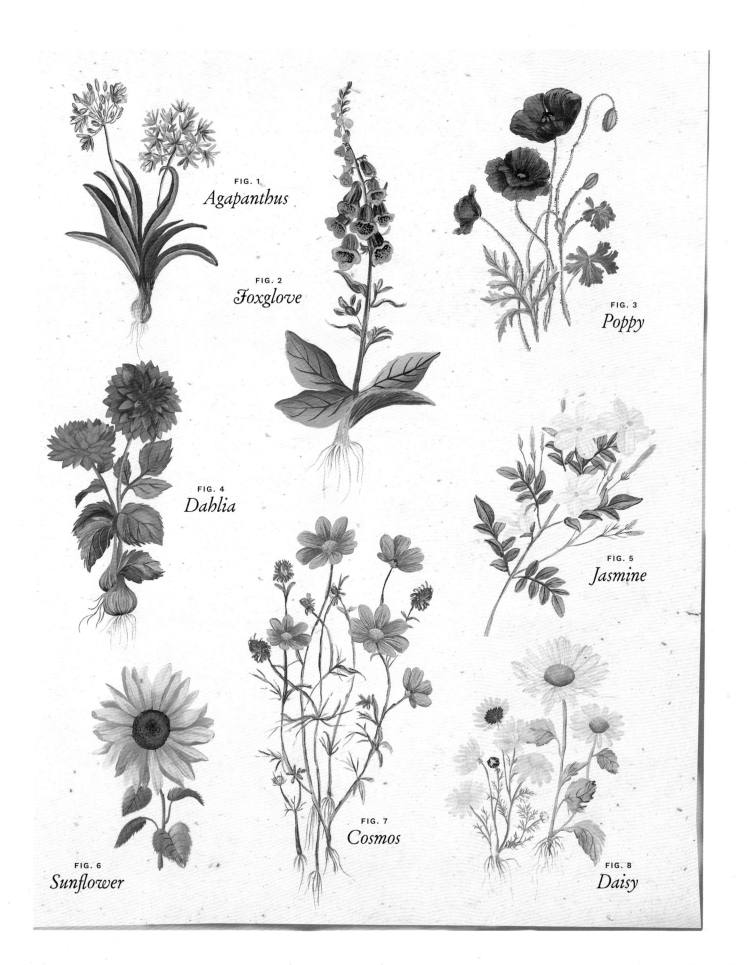

FIG. 1
Agapanthus

FIG. 2
Foxglove

FIG. 3
Poppy

FIG. 4
Dahlia

FIG. 5
Jasmine

FIG. 6
Sunflower

FIG. 7
Cosmos

FIG. 8
Daisy

CHAPTER 4

POWDER
AND COTTON

White

POWDER AND COTTON

Imagine an expanse of freshly fallen snow, a pristine landscape glistening in the sunlight. White represents renewal, an invitation for serenity.

White whispers the delicateness of a flower petal, the lightness of a cloud dancing in the sky, the purity of a moonbeam on a winter's night.

It's the color of silence and introspection, a space for calm and inner peace. White is an invitation for contemplation, a search for simplicity and authenticity.

Part of my garden, called "the white garden," is a French-style oasis of calm. Beds of hydrangeas stand side by side with trimmed hedges, providing calm and tranquility. While white can sometimes make me feel gloomy when it comes to decorating, I must admit that on a table, a bouquet of white flowers in a silver goblet exudes unrivaled elegance—elegance I don't associate with bouquets of white roses, which, I confess, trigger a certain fear in me.

A garden is truly a shared experience that brings great joy to all. That, too, is the power of gardeners. The beauty of nature goes beyond all our expectations, beyond what we may have liked to create ourselves.

"I know gardens where
we forget ourselves, gardens
that teach us, that instruct us
in that silent language
that is made up of nothing
but breath, light, and water.
I listen to these gardens,
I caress them with my eyes,
I feel them living, tirelessly,
like us."

Colette,
Prisons and Paradise (1932)

Leucanthemum vulgare

— DAISY —

The daisy, symbol of simplicity and innocence, has a rich history that dates back to antiquity. Cultivated for its medicinal virtues in the gardens of medieval monasteries, it became a symbol of love in the Middle Ages, when young girls played a game by plucking its petals, chanting: "He loves me, he loves me not." Today, it evokes childhood memories and brings a bucolic spirit to my bouquets, reminding us that beauty often lies in the simplest things.

TYPE — *Perennial*

SOIL — *Rich to neutral*

FLOWERING — *June to October*

Wild grasses, like a carpet of a thousand discoveries, evoke the atmosphere of an English novel. Every year there's a new surprise, like the wind covering the green lawn with petals. The finest florists couldn't create anything more romantic for a wedding. Nature always surpasses us in its strength and beauty.

GARDEN HARVEST

*Apple tree branches, apples, Queen Anne's lace,
hydrangeas, daisies*

The real stars here are these gorgeous baskets designed by
Osanna Visconti for Dior Maison. I let them sit majestically
on my dining room table, which I hate being empty—I find
it depressing. No room should ever be ignored.

I slide chicken wire into my baskets to give the bouquet
the desired shape. I then play with apple tree branches,
hydrangeas, and Queen Anne's lace flowers from my field,
which I poke one after the other into the chicken wire. I leave
the tall branches asymmetrical and place the fallen apples
in the smaller baskets with daisies to add small detail.

The hydrangeas are placed lower down in the baskets
to create different levels.

When you see the whole thing assembled,
it's like looking at a painting.

I often wonder where this passion for watching gardening TV shows and following Instagram accounts exclusively dedicated to flowers and gardening tips comes from. What makes me smile so much is that, in the end, it all creeps into my imagination, into my drawings, into my little Baby Dior designs, and helps me create all the prints that I use in my work.

For some time now, I've been seeing a lot of big-name designers wanting the same thing: huge dahlias, sunflowers, tulips, or even fruits and vegetables adorning prints on the catwalks of the world's biggest brands.

These ladies must have a great influence on us all, providing us with a great source of happiness and hope during these uncertain and sometimes dark times. But, above all, they remind us that the most absolute beauty comes not from ourselves but from nature.

TABLE WITH A VIEW

This is where we usually have a drink, overlooking
the forest that borders one of my flower fields.

On a June evening, I set a table for dinner in front of
my contemplation bench. I picked carrot flowers in the field
and a few greenish-white hydrangeas and daisies. These silver
metal tumblers are always very practical.

It's an impromptu dinner, so I put raffia place mats brought back
from the Philippines on a white tablecloth; it gives a more rustic
feel. I mix white earthenware plates and the vintage lily
of the valley slipware that inspired my designs for Dior.

I place this large bouquet in the middle.

A white table looks as light as the fields before us; a touch
of green adorns the bread plates and old wine glasses. I bring
over blue chairs from the other end of the garden, which work
very well with my bench. I arrange a few cushions to make this
improvised corner comfortable. Candles are simple ivory tapers.

Everything seems to float like a suspended cloud,
and nothing looks heavy.

I'll remove the large bouquet and put it on the small side table,
then I'll place the dish that we'll be sharing in the middle
of the table.

I often create a big bouquet for a *wow* effect,
then I replace it with the food.

Jackie Kennedy loved the understated elegance of roses. She worked with Bunny Mellon to restore the White House Rose Garden, choosing pink and white roses for their simplicity and beauty. These flowers reflected her refined taste and brought a classic touch to official events. Roses are a symbol of grace and purity, traits that Jackie Kennedy embodied throughout her entire life.

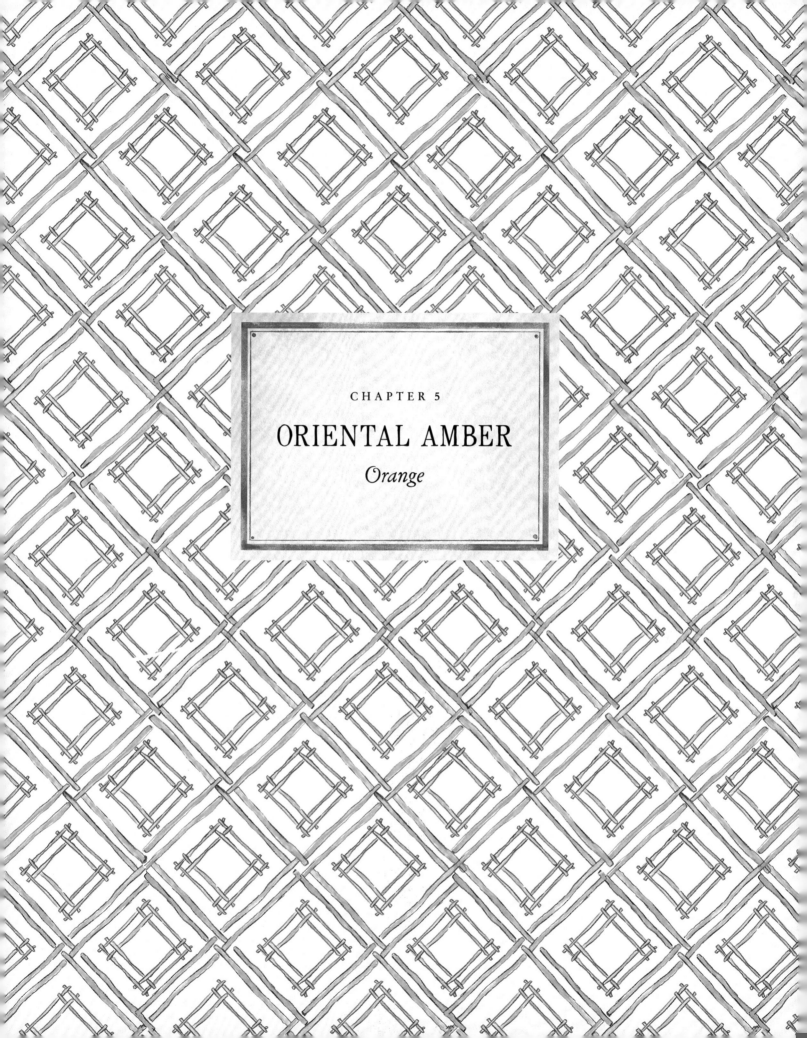

CHAPTER 5

ORIENTAL AMBER

Orange

ORIENTAL AMBER

Orange ignites the horizon in a blazing inferno celebrating the end of the day and the promise of new beginnings. It's the color of the setting sun that envelops the clouds, transforming them into waves of liquid fire: a vibrant warmth that radiates with infectious energy and that warms the heart and soul.

Orange is an explosion of flavors, the juicy sweetness of a ripe orange and the subtle bitterness of citrus zest. It's the intoxicating scent of a field of poppies in bloom, the promise of a spicy, comforting feast.

Orange evokes creativity, enthusiasm, and joie de vivre. It's a fearless, warm color that invites spontaneity and optimism.

I love the boldness of this color and don't like to mix orange with other colors in my bouquets.

Total look only!

Bunny Mellon, a great topiary collector, grew them in her famous garden in Virginia. She saw these plant sculptures as an extension of her love for the structured garden. Elegantly pruned, her topiaries embodied her taste for order, simplicity, and timeless beauty, while adding a personal touch to her green spaces.

Papaver

— POPPY —

The poppy, with its bright red petals, has a rich history. Originating in Eurasia, it spread to fields and farmland. A famous anecdote links it to the First World War, when poppies began to grow up through the debris after the fighting, symbolizing nature's resilience in the face of destruction. The poem "In Flanders Fields," by John McCrae, popularized this association, making the poppy a symbol of peace and remembrance. Today, it serves as a reminder of the ephemeral beauty of life, uniting generations in perseverance and hope.

TYPE *Annual*

SOIL *Limestone & well-drained*

FLOWERING *May to September*

WILD AUTUMN

Rosehips, hydrangeas, dahlias, branches

This bouquet is created like a sculpture, a balancing act
to prevent the vase from tipping over. First, I place the tall
stems and rosehip branches to create a base. I then add three
large hydrangeas, two fairly tall ones and one at the base
of the vase to hide the stems. These beautiful ladies come
and join in the dance. Then I add a few dahlias here and there
to add a splash of color. But not all at the same height.

The branches will add volume and a wild touch!

In the greenhouse, I play with my seedlings, but also with my flowers and potted plants. What could be more practical and decorative than placing a superb geranium on the entrance table? I keep them in the greenhouse and bring them in at the last minute. I do the same thing with small plant pots on an improvised table. I collect old terra-cotta pots because I really don't like them new.

THE ORANGE TREE GREENHOUSE

I take the opportunity to have lunch in my greenhouse
before the days get too hot and I bring out the lemon
and orange trees for the season. What could be better than
dreaming of the Mediterranean and summer ahead of time?

I place a linen tablecloth with ladder stitching on the wooden
work table. Orange trees in their terra-cotta pots recall the world
of the garden and a Dior dinner service I designed, inspired by
my entire citrus collection. It's a pleasure for me to bring
my collections to life in the spaces where I conceived of them.

A few oranges are strewn here and there, as if they had fallen
from the tree; a touch of green neutralizes the power of orange.
Then I add a little terra-cotta and lunch is served. The crystal
glasses are unadorned. Simple.

When I use strong colors like red or orange, I keep the base
very classic so as not to create an overpowering décor.

The most important thing, in living rooms or on tables, is to
provide a feeling of serenity. I think that's what real luxury is all
about. It's not an excess of decorations or flamboyant things,
it's the peace brought by simplicity.

I love hosting lunches and dinners in this greenhouse.

Christmas evening was a unique moment, with a lace tablecloth
in the middle of a snow-covered garden. And another year,
I transformed the greenhouse into a winter living room,
bringing in the garden sofas and covering them with fake fur.

My son Stan's chanterelles

Gently clean 1 pound fresh chanterelles.
Heat 2 tablespoons extra virgin olive oil
in a large frying pan over medium-high
and sauté the chanterelles for 5 to 7
minutes. When they turn golden brown,
add 2 tablespoons unsalted butter,
2 cloves minced garlic, and 1 bunch finely
chopped flat-leaf parsley leaves. Sauté for
a further 2 to 3 minutes. Season with salt
and black pepper and serve immediately.

I often talk about the flowers in my décors, but nature in general also has its place. I like to play with seasonal fruits and vegetables to liven up certain parts of the house. The gourmet aspect appeals to me ... In fact, my Dior collection is based on the couturier's vegetable garden!

A house needs to be welcoming. Pretty bowls of fruit replace a bouquet of flowers on the table: bright red apples fill large vases in the living room, and, in summer, I place bowls of cherries on coffee tables or in the guest bedrooms. Sometimes I fix fruits with lacquer; at Christmas, I paint them gold! I also use pieces of tableware to decorate certain spaces: in the kitchen there are baskets filled with napkins for the whole family, with all the prints mixed together! So everyone knows which one is theirs ...

I like lively homes and as soon as you enter, the ferns announce that this is a house full of life, where nothing is fixed or ever completely in its place.

I play with lots of bouquets in my little tower, using big apple branches, giant hydrangeas, or cherry blossoms. I can stain the floor and feel free. It's also my seed storage, where I number and label them; it's like a science lab. I harvest seeds from certain flowers or I order them. I never thought I'd still be using the pipettes from my school biology class, where I was a mediocre student. Now I'm fascinated by potting soil, watering cans, and the difficulties of plowing, so I'm sure that our land's beautiful soil will allow us to continue producing. This is also where I dry the flowers for my bouquets or spray them with gold at Christmastime. Try spraying alliums. They make lovely decorations for the festive season.

MY FAVORITE FLOWERS

FIG. 1
Amaryllis

Queen of winter flowers, amaryllis unfurls
its petals in brilliant trumpets. Its flamboyant red
illuminates dark days, inviting you to celebrate.
Majestic, it offers a promise of renewal and beauty,
evoking the strength of love and the joy
of reunion, reminding us that even in the cold,
life can blossom brightly.

FIG. 2
Aster

Garden star, the aster lights up autumn with
its shimmering colors. Its delicate flowers dance
in the wind, festooned in shades of violet and
blue. It embodies the softness of golden evenings,
recalling the nostalgia of a season coming to an
end. Its elegant simplicity serves as a confirmation
that beauty persists, even when in decline.

FIG. 3
Japanese Anemone

Nicknamed windflower, the Japanese anemone
quivers in the autumn breeze, like a whisper
of nature. It conjures the ephemeral beauty
of fleeting moments, recalling the fragility of life
and showing strength through its vulnerability.

FIG. 4
Camellia

Pearl of the garden, the camellia blooms
gracefully. Its velvety flowers, in shades of pink,
red, and white, speak sotto voce of softness and
elegance. Its delicate fragrance suggests romance
and timeless beauty, embodying serenity.

FIG. 5
Crocus

Breaking through the snow at the end of winter,
the crocus appears boldly. Its bright yellow, violet,
or white flowers celebrate the return of light.
It heralds milder days and a breath of fresh air
in the garden, reminding us that even small
flowers carry the life force within them
and a promise of new beginnings.

FIG. 6
Colchicum

Jewel of the undergrowth, colchicum emerges
in the murmur of autumn. Its delicate petals,
tinged with violet or pink, open like a well-kept
secret. It recalls the melancholy of shortening days
and is a signal that even in decline, nature offers
glimpses of beauty and promises of renewal.

FIG. 7
Thistle

Proud meadow thorn, the thistle stands boldly,
embellished with bright violet flowers. Its thorns
connote strength in vulnerability. Invoking wild
landscapes, it celebrates the authenticity and
beauty of imperfect things. During my stay
in Scotland, I saw that this was flower everywhere,
marking the landscape.

FIG. 8
Petunia

The jewel of summer gardens, petunia blooms
in cascades of bright colors. Its flowers dance
in the sunlight, offering a spectacle of joy.
Its sweet fragrance elicits memories of laughter
and warmth, reminding us that beauty lies
in simple moments and the bonds of friendship.

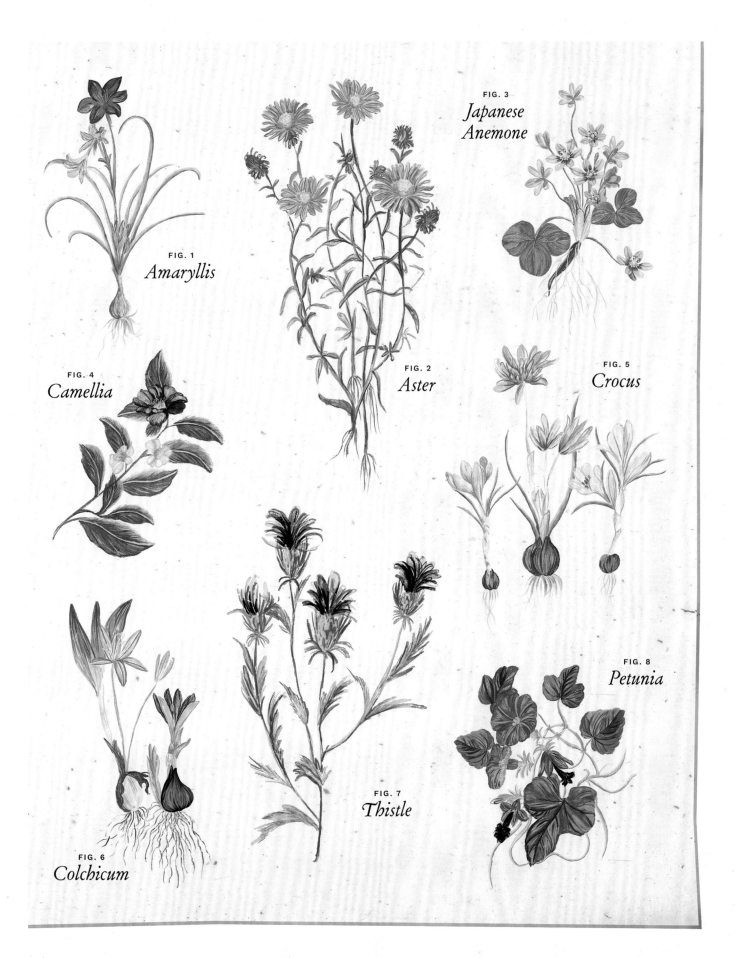

FIG. 1
Amaryllis

FIG. 3
*Japanese
Anemone*

FIG. 4
Camellia

FIG. 2
Aster

FIG. 5
Crocus

FIG. 8
Petunia

FIG. 7
Thistle

FIG. 6
Colchicum

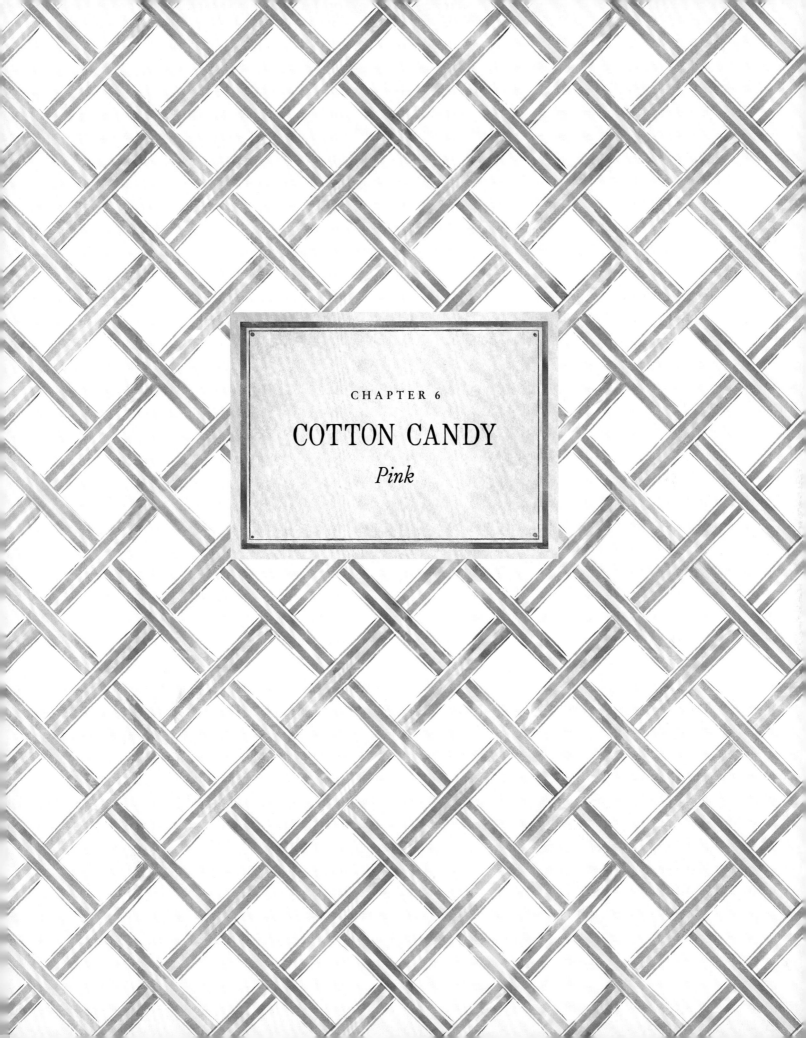

CHAPTER 6

COTTON CANDY

Pink

COTTON CANDY

It's my girly side that I adore: it's Edith Piaf, it's life through rose-tinted glasses, it's Paris, it's joyful, it's feminine, it's romantic, it's the roses in my garden, it's my peonies, it's my only daughter's little outfits, it's the color of Dior, my nail polish collection, and the color of Degas outfits.

I love every shade of pink: candy, bubblegum, cotton candy, shocking, nude, fuchsia, and coral. I mix pinks in my bouquets and on my prints with no limits. I almost want to convince my man to sleep in a pink bedroom. Pink is to be enjoyed without moderation.

I often move the tables to hidden corners of the garden that bloom at different times of the year. I like to surprise people by organizing lunches or dinners in unusual places. I dye the tablecloths with natural flower-based dyes—here, a shocking pink to match the roses in the garden. I love pink and green together. I often use tureens to create centerpieces.

Paeonia

— PEONY —

The peony has fascinated people since ancient times with its lush, fragrant flowers. Indigenous to Asia, Europe, and North America, it was cultivated by the Greeks and Romans for its medicinal properties. Greek myth cites the peony as a creation made in tribute to Paeon, physician to the gods, who used it to cure their wounds. The beautiful nymph Peonia was transformed into a flower by Zeus to escape Apollo's jealousy, thus becoming a symbol of beauty and healing. Today, it evokes love and joy, captivating those who admire it in gardens. I have a garden full of peonies that I treasure. I enjoy them in bouquets without any other flowers. I like to leave these beautiful ladies on their own.

TYPE   *Perennial*

SOIL   *Rich, moist & airy*

FLOWERING   *April to July*

I love working at this stone sink, where I prepare and clean all the flowers from the garden. This door opens onto the garden. Vegetables and fruit are sometimes stored here too, among the flowers. I keep the harvest baskets here as well. I have one for each type of flower and, of course, my pruning shears, which love to disappear!
I have ones made by my friend Willow Crossley and ones I brought back from Japan. Sometimes I leave all the vases here because they look so beautiful together that I dare not separate them.

FEEL GOOD

Wild baby's breath, sweet peas, peonies, brambles

These vases normally sit in my bedroom on a Venetian sideboard that I adore. They mean a lot to me. They're almost like something out of a Proust novel.

I look forward to peonies every season as my little feel-good moment. They're so beautiful and make me smile. I arrange them in my vases in shades of pink or raspberry. Their color palette always adds drama to the table.

I add a few sweet peas, brambles, and wild baby's breath to give my arrangements an airy feel. I always use one or three "star" flowers per vase!

We spend a lot of time in the countryside and often set out big tables for friends and "children" who aren't really children anymore. I place big tables in the field with candles, and we have music playing. Nothing really matches, neither the plates nor the chairs … It's a happy mess. A few vases of flowers and large tablecloths don't distract from the beautiful view. It's informal and often very cheerful.

GREEK EASTER

I am Greek and Orthodox. The tradition of Easter is very
important to us. There were actually ten of us that day,
but I took a less crowded photo before setting the table for real.

I suppose I wanted to see life through rose-tinted glasses
at that point in time.

It's a soft color that puts a smile on your face, even though
it is very feminine.

An egg-shaped bouquet is presented in the family soup
tureen like a sculpture. We could have made it in chocolate,
which I do some years.

A very pale pink note accentuates an old embroidered tablecloth;
touches of silverware that I love to use make the table look chic.

A few seasonal flowers from the garden sit in silver bud vases,
of course. Cherry branches always bring a dancing, poetic feel to
the table. These recall the plates I designed for Dior during a trip
to Japan, following in the footsteps of Christian Dior himself.

I created a contrast with cutlery that bears no relation
to the rest of the table, and I also added a few chocolates
for a gourmand's touch.

But Easter tables can quickly turn into a Disney scene!
Even though I love Mickey's world.

Small individual butter dishes add a special detail, and little
vintage doilies under each water glass remind me of Queen
Victoria's beautiful tables. When you use beautiful objects,
there's no point in overdoing it.

Water glasses should always be filled—it looks more
inviting—and napkins should never be too flat.

Often, each table at home is different.
I play around with my tablecloths
and services, depending on the flowers
in the garden. Decorating the tables
with flowers is the part I enjoy the most.
I love to take my time and savor it.

I place objects on the tables and invent
according to my mood. Sometimes
I let Mom, Isabelle, or Catherine take over.

The table on the right is Mom's. She loves
pink, roses, and the garden. Nature comes
alive like that. I think it's a great success;
it's where our worlds come together.
Mom succeeded in refining a soft,
elegant fantasy here.

I preferred to set the other tables,
which are much more serious,
in a small format.

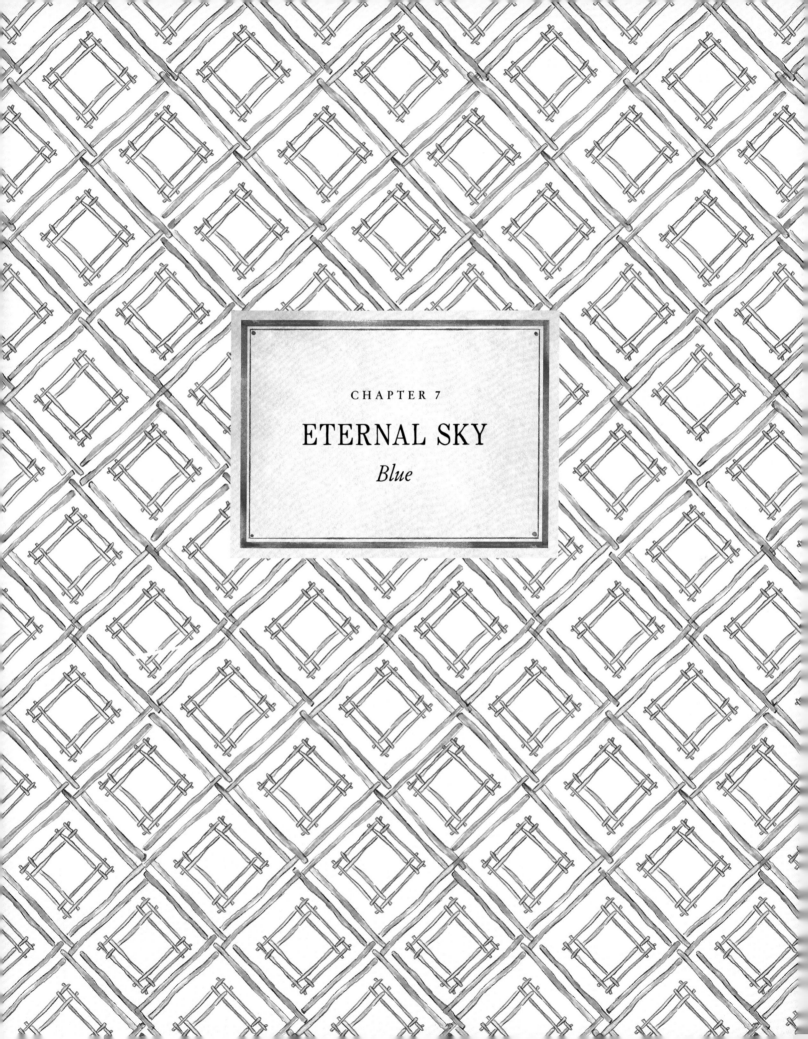

CHAPTER 7

ETERNAL SKY

Blue

ETERNAL SKY

Blue. Vast as a cloudless summer sky and deep as the ocean that stretches as far as the eye can see. It is the serenity of a mountain lake in the early morning when the air is pure and the world is slowly waking up.

Blue whispers stories of faraway journeys, waves dancing in the wind, and starry skies on a summer night. It's the promise of a cool breeze on your face, a dip in crystal-clear water, a sense of calm and freedom.

Blue is the color of the imagination, the color that transports us to distant dreams and invites us to explore the farthest reaches of our minds.

Blue is by far my favorite color for bedroom wallpaper, whether in floral prints or stripes. I find the combination of blue and white with wicker or silverware absolutely chic. Sometimes I like to mix it with green, as these two colors work divinely together.

The greenhouse in the middle of the flower
field is where I sort and clean my cosmos,
dahlias, daisies, poppies, and sunflowers.
This is where buckets of picked flowers
are prepared and sent off to
my Coffee Flower Shop.

Christian Dior's lily of the valley is embossed
on my day-to-day tableware. When the
objects are understated and of very high
quality, I like to have fun by adding
a touch of fantasy, like this blend
of flowers and colors.

"After women, flowers are the most divine
creations."—Christian Dior

Delphinium

— DELPHINIUM —

The delphinium is also known as dolphinelle and is remarkable for its bright colors: blue, purple, pink or white. It takes its name from the Greek *delphis*, meaning "dolphin," an analogy to the dolphin's snout. In the past, it was often planted to ward off scorpions; today, it is highly prized in gardens for its ability to attract pollinators. Native Americans also used it to create a blue dye. The delphinium is considered a symbol of protection, although it also represents lightness, grace, and dignity.

TYPE	*Perennial*
SOIL	*Rich & well-drained*
FLOWERING	*June to August*

A garden table set in the middle of the lawn under the magnolia tree. Around it, tall grasses form a bubble that surrounds us. We call the large boxwood composition "cloud." It's the signature of landscape designer Milan Hajsinek, and it needs a lot of maintenance, but I must say that the interplay between the wild grasses and the boxwood structure is sensational. The table is simple. My plates, with their embossed canework motif from the House of Dior, are set on a tablecloth from my favorite place in Venice … I love checks on everyday tables! They're stylish and easy to find. My friend Willow Crossley's bud vases make the delicate garden flowers dance, and the glasses are from Zara!

A pesticide-free garden requires a lot of attention. A garden makes our hands and clothes really dirty, but I always make sure that I have clean vases, baskets, tools, and work areas. My top assistant is Vadim, my youngest son, who has had two very green thumbs and a great love of nature ever since he was a small child.

SOFT BOUQUET IN A PINEAPPLE

Poppies, delphiniums, sweet peas, pincushion flowers,
Queen Anne's lace, lady's mantle

It's rare that I combine so many flowers. This happens when I don't want to take too much from the garden and the flower field I use for cut flowers is still between growing seasons.

Here and there, I use baby blue delphiniums, a big bunch of Queen Anne's lace, which I always enjoy using, some baby pink pincushions, sweet peas, and poppies in soft pastel colors.

I start by placing the delphiniums high up, weaving in Queen Anne's lace to create volume, and poke in the other guests here and there. A few sweet peas droop slightly, and I let them express themselves with great natural flair.

P.S.: Fill the vase with plenty of water for the tall stems.

A collection of hats, a collection of vases, and the room where I like to make my bouquets on Saturdays, when everyone else is asleep. There are lots of baskets, vases, and hats here, but never enough. I think they always look pretty in a country house.

Florence Grinda, who gave me my first job at Emanuel Ungaro and who has amazing taste, had baskets hanging in her kitchen, covering the whole ceiling. I left with that image in my head and told myself that one day I'd do the same!

" Je vous conseillerais de porter des fleurs comme des œillets ou des bleuets "

5.

Œillet

RIMBAUD'S BLUE TABLE

Blue is like a pair of jeans—it pretty much works
with everything. There's no point in only matching it with white,
even though I must say I love this combination,
it's so easy and perfect.

The tableware here is decorated with a fine black line
illustration. I take a risk putting flowers on flowers, but you have
to try. Just take a photo and see if it works. The image will tell
you immediately if you've crossed the line or not.

Small blue earthenware vases with a few flowers are placed
around my living room. I scatter them about the table, without
adding too much, as there are already a lot of floral patterns here.

I accentuate the touch of black with the cutlery and mismatch
the water glasses to create the little not-so-perfect table trick.
Otherwise it would be boring and bland.

I love this double page, and I'll explain why.

Of course, I love this picture of us three, Vadim, Clélia, and I.

My house, like those of our grandmothers, is full of toile de Jouy. I love these prints because, lying in my bed, I could imagine so many things looking at these walls full of scenes …

These prints are also treasured by the House of Dior, and here they are on my Baby Dior models posing on the bed in my bedroom. My son Vadim is exactly as he appears— an adorable little boy who gets into lots of mischief.

I place my mini topiaries, pinched from Bunny Mellon and found by Milan, on my tables or in the hallway.

This particular Christmas at Dior, everything was blue, white, and gold. It was fun to play the very sweet card of Christian Dior's flowers in blue and white, like wallpaper in a young girl's bedroom. Just like his beloved little sister's might have been. The gold and gingerbread added a magic touch. I must say, I love using blue and gold together at Christmas, even a deep midnight blue.

CHAPTER 8

PASSIONATE
RED

Red

PASSIONATE RED

Red fascinates me. I don't know if I like red, but it arouses emotions in me. Ultimately, just as in life, the emotion that certain things provoke is maybe stronger than whether you like them or not.

Red is dangerous and dramatic, often inviting passionate and captivating love. It has represented power and majesty since the Middle Ages. In painting, it was the first color to be used and is the richest, both socially and artistically.

Red flowers are very cheeky and I rarely mix them with others, often using shades of raspberry or plum. I also enjoy combining them with soft pink, allowing me to calm them down in their majestic success!

It often makes my teams smile when I suddenly introduce this color into a collection.

Papaver Somniferum

— DANISH FLAG POPPY —

The Danish Flag poppy, with its white flowers and black center, is reminiscent of the Danish flag and has a fascinating history linked to Scandinavian culture. In Viking times, according to legend, Danish warriors planted poppies on battlefields to honor the souls of fallen soldiers. These flowers have become a symbol of memory and bravery, recalling the sacrifice of ancestors. Today, the Danish Flag poppy is prized in Danish gardens, providing a touch of poetry and color while evoking national pride and past struggles. Poppies are one of my favorite flowers—I adore their pop of color and their stems. They look like sculptures, and I love them in my compositions.

TYPE   *Annual*

SOIL   *Well-drained*

FLOWERING   *June to October*

Roses d'Hiver

My Christmas is full of nature. The forest, branches, and a touch of pink to avoid always being too obviously red. Pink mixes marvelously with red. I bring out velvet ribbons, which are never wide enough. I dip my roses or fruit in wax. The charm of Christmas lies in making things with your hands and, above all, having fun. Be kitsch and chic, it's now or never! I prefer single-flower bouquets. I've always had a penchant for leaving the ladies to themselves; it gives them strength.

COUTURE BOUQUET

Dahlias, nerine lilies, privet, Japanese anemones

I love blue and white vases. I like them when they're empty,
as ornaments or filled with flowers. I could have whole
collections of them. Once, for Kate Moss, I designed a table
covered with these vases, full of flowers from the English
countryside. Sometimes, I'll place a large one on the table
and put its smaller cousins around it, or a little brother from
the same family next to it, with just one flower or a few stems.
I play with my dahlias, their height and shape, like sculptures.
A few stems from the forest bring a little disorder. Then, I'll add
a flower, often from another family, if the others are willing.

Here, the fiery, passionate hues are peppered with candy-pink,
bubblegum, plum, and raspberry, adding depth
to the arrangement.

The Japanese anemones at their base add a delicate touch.

ODE TO BEAUTY

I love September evenings of soft, golden light.

I like the idea of subtly conveying the atmosphere around a table,
even if it is set in a simple way for a few friends. I like dinners
for four to six guests animated by a single central conversation.

A romantic candlelit dinner under the fifteenth-century vault.
This arch has fascinated me since the first day in this house.

Color gradients on tables are pretty: pink linen placed
under my grandmother's slightly transparent organdy
tablecloth announces the dahlias' raspberry palette
and the burgundy plates.

A range of pink, raspberry, red currant, and red adds nuance
to the table. Matching glasses present different shades
of the same color. Silverware and a few tumblers of flowers give
the table a very festive look, and the large central candlestick
replaces the candlesticks from the dining room.

Tip: Play with color palettes. Otherwise, my white tablecloth
would clash with the wooded part of the garden
and the warm-colored dishes.

The candlestick should be high and the flowers low
to allow friends to see one another and talk across the table.
Cover the candles in windy weather.

Light up the surrounding garden with lanterns and add
a touch of classical music on a small portable speaker.

I have a wonderful neighbor, Karine, who runs a flea market and finds baskets for me every week. I also buy them in Gerberoy, a village known for the beauty of its gardens and its rose festival. There, you can find a basket maker whose creations I adore. I sell many in my Coffee Flower Shop. Vintage, of course! If you're mad about gardens, you should visit this French village, especially in spring!

STRAWBERRY CAKE

A multilayered strawberry cake is a bit like a pyramid of indulgence. Each tier rises gently, generously topped with light cream and bright strawberries. The strawberries, like rubies in sugared lace, provide that irresistible freshness. It's a dessert that calls for a celebration, and we cut into each slice with wonder, as if discovering treasure. When it sits on the table, there's no need for words, just the desire to savor this suspended moment.

SERVES 6

Sponge cake
Unsalted butter for pan
1 cup (120 g) all-purpose flour, sifted, plus more for pan
4 eggs, separated
Pinch of salt
½ cup (120 g) granulated sugar

Crème mousseline
1 vanilla pod
1¼ cups (300 ml) whole milk
3 egg yolks
⅓ cup (70 g) granulated sugar
¼ cup (30 g) cornstarch
1 stick plus 2 tablespoons (150 g) unsalted butter, cubed, at room temperature

Assembly
1 pound (500 g) fresh strawberries
2 tablespoons granulated sugar (for macerating), if needed
Water-sugar syrup, to soak sponge cake
Confectioners' sugar and edible flower petals for decorating (optional)

MAKE THE SPONGE CAKE
Preheat the oven to 350°F (180°C). Butter and flour a 9-inch round cake pan.

In a medium bowl, combine the egg whites and salt and whisk until stiff. In a large bowl, whisk the yolks with the sugar until the mixture whitens.

Gently fold the flour into the yolk-sugar mixture. Very gently fold in the stiffly beaten egg whites so they don't deflate.

Pour the batter into the prepared pan and bake until the cake springs back when gently pressed, 15 to 20 minutes.

MAKE THE CRÈME MOUSSELINE
Split the vanilla bean and scrape out the seeds, putting both pod and seeds in a medium saucepan. Stir in the milk and set over medium heat to warm.

In a medium bowl, whisk the egg yolks with the sugar until frothy, then whisk in the cornstarch.

Pour the hot milk over the mixture while whisking constantly, then return the mixture to the saucepan and thicken on a low heat while continuing to whisk.

Once thickened, remove from the heat, stir in half the butter, and let cool to room temperature. Once the crème mousseline has cooled, add the remaining butter and whisk until smooth and light.

ASSEMBLE THE CAKE
Wash, hull, and halve the strawberries. Taste one; if they are not sweet enough to your liking, put them in a bowl and sprinkle with the sugar. Refrigerate for 30 minutes. Set aside some of the halved strawberries to decorate the cake. Leave the others halved or cut them into smaller pieces for the cake layers.

Cut the cooled sponge cake into 2 or 3 layers, according to your preference. Use a pastry brush to dab a little syrup on each layer of sponge cake.

Place one cake layer on a large plate or cake stand. Spread some of the crème mousseline on top, then arrange some of the halved or chopped strawberries on top. Repeat for each layer. Top the cake with a final layer of crème mousseline and decorate with the strawberries that were set aside.

Place the strawberry cake in the refrigerator for at least 2 hours so that it sets.

Before serving, decorate with a dusting of confectioners' sugar and edible flower petals, if desired.

MY FAVORITE FLOWERS

FIG. 1
Christmas Clematis

Star of the festive season, the Christmas clematis
is decorated with delicate, beguiling flowers.
Its white or purple petals light up the winter with
their grace. It evokes the magic of celebration,
bringing a comforting softness. In the cold,
it reminds us that beauty can blossom
and that hope of renewal is always present.

FIG. 2
Winter Heather

Resilient, winter heather blooms gracefully
in the cold. Its pink or purple bells add a splash
of color to frozen landscapes, a signal that even
gloomy days can carry bursts of beauty.

FIG. 3
Hellebore

The flower of mystery, hellebore emerges elegantly
from the shadows. Its delicate pale green petals
brighten the frozen ground with their discreet
charm. A symbol of hope and resilience, it recalls
that even in darkness, beauty can spring forth
and bring comfort.

FIG. 4
Grape Hyacinth

Combined with its bewitching fragrance, for me,
grape hyacinth evokes responsibility and self-
confidence. Its bunches of blue, mauve, pink
or white bells brighten up any garden.

FIG. 5
Bearberry

Pearl of the undergrowth, the bearberry blooms
with delicacy. Its subtle fragrance provides
a soothing sweetness. It evokes the simplicity
of nature, reminding us that treasures are hidden
in unassuming places. Its evergreen leaves
symbolize fidelity and constancy, bringing life
throughout the year.

FIG. 6
Magnolia

The bewitchingly beautiful magnolia unfurls
its large pink and white flowers. Its fragrance
evokes the softness of summer days. It majestically
illuminates the garden like a symbol of love and
dignity. In its velvety petals, it captures tenderness
and is a tribute to the notion that beauty can exist
in the ephemeral.

FIG. 7
Paperwhite Narcissus

With its trumpet-like petals, paperwhite narcissus
awakens, illuminating gardens with its white
light. Its fragrance evokes gentleness and rebirth,
bringing a breath of fresh air to sunny days.
In its delicate grace, it embodies hope and reminds
us that every moment is precious, celebrating
the renewal of nature.

FIG. 8
Snowdrop

Winter messenger, the snowdrop emerges
from beneath the snow. Its tiny white bell-shaped
flowers promise rebirth. It announces the arrival
of spring, celebrating the awakening of life
and signals that even in winter, beauty can bloom.

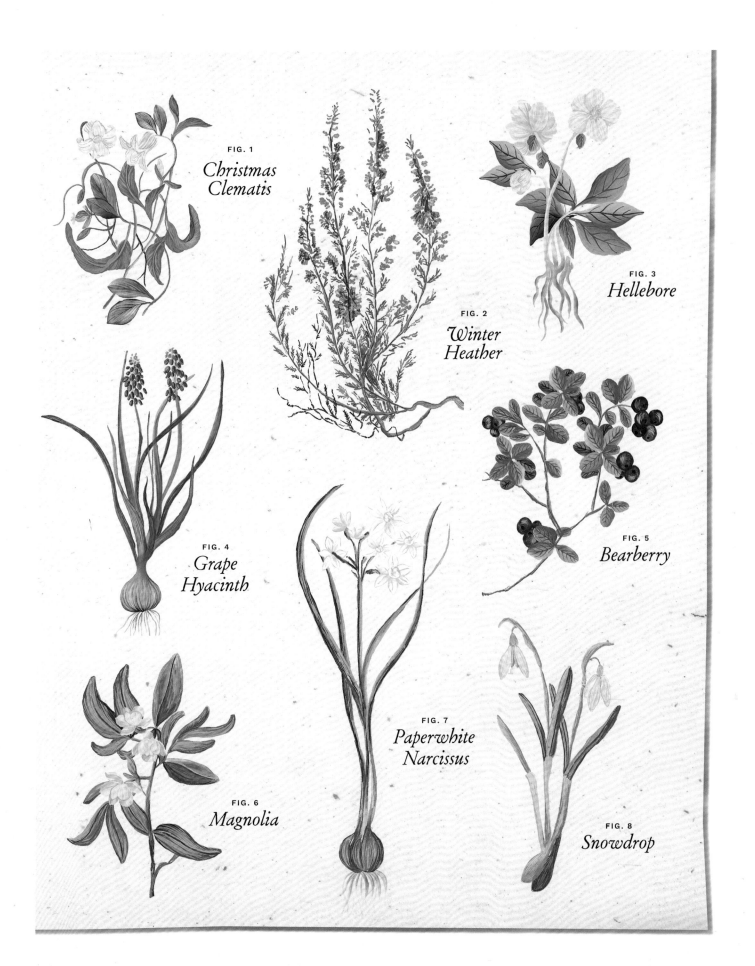

FIG. 1
Christmas Clematis

FIG. 2
Winter Heather

FIG. 3
Hellebore

FIG. 4
Grape Hyacinth

FIG. 5
Bearberry

FIG. 6
Magnolia

FIG. 7
Paperwhite Narcissus

FIG. 8
Snowdrop

PASSIONATE RED

ACKNOWLEDGMENTS

I've always worked in a team. If people think I do a lot of things, it's because
I have fairies around me. Thank you from the bottom of my heart.

Thank you, Billal, for these shared moments and for your eye on this book.

Catherine, my editor at Rizzoli New York, for mothering me so patiently,
and her team of course.

Thank you, Oleg, for your sublime photos and so many years
of working together.

Sanaz, of course I don't need to introduce you. Thank you for always
making things happen!

Thank you, Marie, who has put a crazy amount of energy
into this book, and Béa, for many hours sorting out the images.
To my studio, Natacha for her artist's hands and Lucie for hers!

To superwoman Isabelle and her men, Laurent, Jimmy, and Cyprien
in the countryside, who can do the shoots without me now, with the help
of Valentin who knows how to work miracles, assisted by Babette,
always helpful, and Marcella, the best at Christmas wreaths.

Marie, my dream florist with her team and Salomé, for finding solutions
for me when the flowers were in the spotlight!

Edoardo for these sublime bulbs that give me sublime flowers.

Milan Hajsineck for this dream garden and his incredible talent.

Éric Chauvin, the world's greatest florist, and his team
for their incomparable and unique talents.

Lila and my neighbor Karine, for hunting
with such a beautiful eye for my garden.

The maison Thevenon for printing my flowers for eternity.

My teams at Dior: my studio, Camille, Suse, Élodie, Élodie Lan,
and Tiffany for their support in my ravings; Shéhérazade, who never breaks
when faced with a challenge; Marion, for keeping her keen eye on the book.

The House of Dior and the Arnault family, especially Delphine,
for their trust over the last fourteen years.

Olivier, who always guides me and with whom I learn so much.

The entire Dior communications team for their support.

Thank you, Mom, for being the muse in my life.

All my family, thank you for celebrating Christmas in September
for so many years; for putting up with your mom's crazy ideas!
Stan and Andreas—for knowing how to cook and count for me—
I promise to do the same for your passions!

FLOWER COUTURE

From My Garden to My House

First published in the United States of America in 2025
by Rizzoli International Publications, Inc.
49 West 27th Street
New York, NY 10001
www.rizzoliusa.com

Text: Cordelia de Castellane
Photography: Billal Taright

Except for pages :
10–11, 46, 54, 55, 61 (top right), 75, 79, 119 (bottom left), 134 (bottom left), 183, 200: Dean Hearne; 23, 28–29,
56 (top left), 65 (top left), 90 (top left and right), 91, 93, 101, 107, 118, 119 (top and bottom right), 129, 144, 145,
155 (bottom right), 157, 161, 165, 180, 184 (top and bottom right), 186–187, 189, 193 (top and bottom right), 204,
206–207, 209 (top left), 213 (top and bottom right), 217, 222 (top left and right), 232 : Oleg Covian; 34 (top left):
David Biedert; 34 (top right), 35, 47, 56 (bottom left and right), 57 (top right), 77 (bottom left), 80, 81, 90
(bottom right), 106 (top left and right), 170, 172, 173, 176, 177, 192, 193 (top and bottom left), 202 (top left),
213 (bottom left), 219 (top left and right), 226 (bottom left), 233 (top left): Cordelia de Castellane; 34 (bottom right),
65 (top right), 106 (bottom right), 110 (top left), 209 (top right), 212, 213 (top left): all rights reserved; 56 (top right),
84, 85, 106 (bottom left), 126, 134 (top left and bottom right), 203, 233 (bottom right): Milan Hajsinek;
65 (bottom left), 130 (top left): Anaïs Barelli; 90 (bottom left), 155 (top left): Charlotte Robin; 209 (bottom left):
Adeline Mai; 210–211: Skiss Agency.

Publisher: Charles Miers
Editorial Direction: Catherine Bonifassi
Production Manager: Maria Pia Gramaglia
Managing Editor: Lynn Scrabis
Translator: Emma Sroussi
Copyeditor and Proofreader: Tricia Levi

Design: Drink Studio - Pierre Boisson

Editorial Coordination:
CASSI EDITION
Vanessa Blondel, Cyriane Flamant, Candice Guillaume

ISBN: 978-0-8478-4778-5
Library of Congress Control Number: 2024946097
Printed in Italy
2025 2026 2027 2028 / 10 9 8 7 6 5 4 3 2 1

Visit us online:
Instagram.com/RizzoliBooks
Facebook.com/RizzoliNewYork
X: @Rizzoli_Books
Youtube.com/user/RizzoliNY